CORNISH
BORN & BREWED

A Family Tradition

The Story of St Austell Brewery, 1851-2011

written by Liz Luck

I feel no pain dear mother now
But oh, I am so dry!
O take me to a brewery
And leave me there to die.

St Austell Brewery 2011

First published in Great Britain in 2001. Revised version published in 2011 by
St Austell Brewery Co. Ltd, 63 Trevarthian Road, St Austell, Cornwall PL25 4BY

© St Austell Brewery Co. Ltd

ISBN 978-0-9540537-1-0

Contents

Walter and Hester in the garden of The Brake
The Seven Stars, St Austell, Walter Hicks's first pub
Walter Hicks invoice from 1890, courtesy of Cornwall Records Office
The copper, 1914-1998

Adam Luck, Estate Director; Jonathan Neame, non-executive Director; Gerard Barnes, non-executive Director;

Foreword

So here we are again ten years on, celebrating 160 years of St Austell Brewery in 2011. The last decade, since we published the original copy of Liz Luck's *Brewing for Cornwall* to celebrate our 150th birthday, has proved to be a particularly exciting time for everyone involved with the Brewery. I am pleased to report that the Company remains on a strong financial footing and has benefited from a period of significant investment and growth in all areas.

When you see the highlights of recent years documented as they are in the last chapter, it makes me feel very proud of our achievements. None of these successes would have been possible without the support of our employees, licensees and customers. Their loyalty is crucial to our business and I would like to take this opportunity to thank them - One and All - for their tremendous support which makes St Austell Brewery the success it is today.

If I had to pick out one highlight over recent years it would be the reputation of the quality of our beers which has been transformed, with Tribute leading the way. We start the next decade with an exciting new range of beers that we hope will keep the brewhouse busy for many a year to come. In addition, our pub estate, our free trade business and our national sales have all adapted successfully in the last decade to meet the demands of a fast-changing market place, and today they now bring the St Austell Brewery name to more customers than ever before.

St Austell Brewery remains at heart a family business and it has been very gratifying to welcome more descendants of our founder Walter Hicks to the Company, both on the Board and in the workforce.

Will Michelmore, who joined us as a non-executive Director in 1996, was appointed non-executive Chairman in 2008, succeeding Piers Thompson who became our Honorary President in recognition of 46 years loyal service to the Company. Gerard Barnes joined the Board as a non-executive Director in 2005, while Piers Thompson junior is National Sales Manager and Humphrey Voelcker has just joined us as Estate Surveyor having worked at Savills, London for the last ten years.

I consider myself very fortunate to be part of such a great family company and privileged to be Managing Director. The next ten years promise to be as eventful as the last decade and I am confident that, as we work from a strong foundation, we are well placed to continue to meet the challenges the industry faces but, at the same time grow and thrive over the years ahead.

The vision for the future remains the same - a happy and fulfilled team working together for the good of the Company, our customers and the South West region as a whole.

Cheers!

James Staughton
Managing Director

Walter Hicks, *founder of St Austell Brewery*

Introduction

Who was Walter Hicks, and why should we remember him? The name might be familiar to devotees of a strong Cornish ale called Hicks Special Draught, they might even have noticed its pump clip which for many years bore the slightly melancholy image of a sombre bearded man with a high starched Victorian collar, but as to who he was – well what does it matter, as long as the beer tastes good?

The First and Last Inn, Sennen. Leased to the Brewery from 1935-1978

Cornwall was an extraordinary place to be in the early nineteenth century, and much of the structure of our lives today has its origins in this period which was a ferment of energy and innovation. Philip Payton, in his definitive history *Cornwall* describes it thus: *'The heady mix of Trevithick and Davy, Lemon and Fox, Basset and Williams, Treffry and Gilbert, Bickford and Gurney, made for an astonishing concentration of intellectual activity and inventiveness… Cornish society became remarkably self-confident and assertive, and Cornishness was expressed increasingly in terms of technological and scientific advance.'* He goes on to describe how a new breed of Cornish industrialist emerged alongside the practical engineers: *'These industrialists - capitalists, innovators, inventors, reformers - brought a particular single mindedness and determination which prompted the redefinition of Cornish society as modern and progressive, and which helped mould a re-defining Cornish identity based on industrial prowess'.*

Out of this intoxicating crucible came Walter Hicks: not an extraordinary man, no visionary or genius, but the embodiment of his age - he was Typical Victorian Man and he was going to Found something.

The business he founded, on the principles of sound finance, paternalistic care for his workforce and a fascination with cutting-edge industrial technology, is today one of Cornwall's leading private companies. It directly employs some 1,000 people, owns 168 public houses and hotels in Cornwall, Devon and Somerset and has an annual turnover of almost £100 million, yet it remains as it has always been at heart, a family concern. It strides the national stage as one of just a handful of vigorous and independent regional breweries to survive the years of take-over and amalgamation which almost killed off the traditional brewery. Locally it is a beneficiary of, as well as a contributor to, the cultural distinctiveness of Cornwall. No company so closely identified with such a high-profile, recognisable region of Britain could fail to benefit from the association, but it has also added to Cornwall's reputation for distinction and quality through its intrinsic commitment to high standards and a strong visual and local identity.

The business he founded has been called St Austell Brewery since 1934, but 160 years ago it had no name; it was simply a young Cornishman called Walter Hicks malting barley in a shed at Trenance.

Map of Lower Menadue Farm, 1842

Chapter I
The Beginnings, 1851-1900

Walter's early life is somewhat obscure. He was baptised at Luxulyan Church on January 30th 1829, the first-born son of a 75-year-old yeoman farmer called Richard Hicks and his second wife Frances (née Warn). Richard and Frances lived at Lower Menadue, then a large farming settlement on the rough rocky fringes of moorland between Bugle and Luxulyan, clustered on the lower slopes of the hill from which it took its Cornish name (*meneth du* – the Black Hill).

Modern replacement of the old memorial tablet in Luxulyan Church

There had been Hickses at Menadue for many generations. This was never rich farming land – A.L. Rowse described it as *'typical Celtic country of scattered holdings cultivating a little of the waste around them, gradually breaking in the unrewarding soil'* – but there was always an extra living to be made from streaming for tin in the shallow valley bottoms, and there is evidence to suggest that at one time the family had achieved some social status. *Lake's Parochial History* (1867-73) refers to an old memorial tablet in Luxulyan Church (*'now nearly obliterated'*) commemorating a Walter Hicks, gentleman of Menadue who died in July 1636, and bearing the arms of the Hicks family described as *'Or, a castle triple towered between three battle axes sable'*.

Richard Hicks's first marriage, to his father's housekeeper Elizabeth Pascoe, had been childless and perhaps it was with a mixture of relief and some surprise that he swiftly married Frances Warn on November 13th 1828, not long before the birth of his son. Walter was just six years old, however, and his sister Frances Bersey Hicks three, when his father died in February 1835. What happened to Walter after this is not entirely clear but it seems likely that he never again lived permanently at his ancestral home, which was subsequently farmed by tenants. A year later his mother married a man called John Miller, and went on to have two more children whilst living at Bridges in Luxulyan. The 1841 census return, however, records Walter and Frances Hicks aged twelve and nine and mysteriously described as 'independent', living with the Nicholls family at Lestoon on the other side of the valley from Menadue; the Millers are not to be found. The Nicholls family was related to Walter through his grandfather, and this would fit in with the Hicks family tradition which has it that both Walter's father and mother died when he was young and thereafter he was cared for by assorted aunts.

The next time Walter reappears in our view is in the 1851 census as a young man of 22. Now he is living as a boarder at Trenance Farm to the north-west of St Austell, on the high ridge of land between the Gover and Trenance valleys. Walter's landlady was Phillipa Andrew, widow of George Andrew and described as a farmer of 166 acres; also amongst the household at Trenance at that time was her 13-year-old step-daughter Caroline who was later to become Walter's second wife.

Walter is described in the census as a landed proprietor, but shortly afterwards, probably in the autumn of 1851, he set up in business as a maltster. It is clear that the Andrew family (sometimes written 'Andrews') had a significant influence on Walter's life; not only did he marry two of them – first cousins – but it

Caroline Hicks, née Andrew

The Beginnings, 1851-1900

is also likely that it was their involvement in the malting business as well as farming (George and Henry Andrew were registered as maltsters in Fore Street in 1844 and 1847) that led Walter to venture into this particular profession. Family tradition has it that to finance the endeavour he took out a mortgage of £1500 on Lower Menadue, probably with the East Cornwall Bank (Robins, Foster, Coode and Bolitho, later to become Barclays) in St Austell. The exact location of Walter's first malt house is unknown, but was somewhere in the Trenance area – either at the farm or nearby in the valley.

There is no evidence to suggest that Walter was brewing at this stage, but as he would have supplied malt to many of the ale-houses and inns in and around St Austell which brewed their own beer, no doubt he was gaining valuable insights into the business. Within ten years Walter had married Emma, daughter of St Austell draper Benjamin Andrew, and moved his business to Church Street in the centre of the town, just down from the White Hart Hotel. By now he was trading as a wine merchant as well as a maltster, and it was not long before he had driven his local competitors (initially six maltsters and three wine and spirit merchants) out of business.

Walter might well have first tried his hand at the art of brewing in 1863 after buying the lease of the Seven Stars Inn, with its own small brew house, but it seems likely that his sights had always been set on building St Austell's first modern commercial-scale brewery. Within a year he had begun the long and tortuous process of buying the old London Inn on Market Street; due to its complicated shared ownership it was a process that was to take him until 1870 to complete. This site was worth waiting for: the inn itself had sixteen rooms, a large cellar, a brew house, yard, stable and loft, but the extensive site he eventually secured also included land running uphill towards the station, where he later built Tregarne House, and property on Market Hill which he was to use for offices and a malt house. In 1869 he began to build his new Steam Brewery and a house for his growing family, on the main site of the London Inn just up the hill from the parish church.

'At the foot of Menacuddle Hill started an institution of which St Austell has reason to be proud, Walter Hicks's brewery. As a regrettable teetotaller I cannot personally witness to the excellence of its beverages, as to which there is better and consistent testimony from all over Cornwall. But the heavy, sweet, soporific odour of hops and malt from the brewery up the hill is a constant reminder of schooldays, as I find is the case with many others beside me – there is nothing so nostalgic as scents and smells.'

A.L. Rowse *St Austell: Church, Town and Parish* (1960)

The grand building, with its classical brick façade and rows of identical round-headed windows fronting Market Street, is known today as Tregonissey House. You can still recognise certain features that identify its origins as a brewery, including the

Tregonissey House

louvered ventilation lantern on the roof ridge and a distinctively massive chimney. In using steam to heat the mash instead of direct heating by furnaces (hence the proud appellation 'Steam Brewery') and a new form of refrigeration system, Walter Hicks took advantage of the innovations in the brewing industry that swept the country in the 1870s. There is no doubt that his enthusiasm

Malting

Malt is where it all begins. Barley is one of the four crucial ingredients in the brewing of traditional British beers, along with hot water ('liquor'), hops and yeast. The malting process enables the carbohydrate in the barley to be easily released so that fermentation may then convert it to alcohol.

After drying, the barley is screened to give even sized grains & to remove dust

Traditional malt houses of this period needed a large well-ventilated floor area and a strong construction to support the weight of tanks filled with liquid. Walter's first malt house might have been a small operation, but it would have been an easily recognisable building with a long, low profile, repetitive fenestration and a distinctive, perhaps conical, kiln roof.

The process involves steeping the barley in water for up to 70 hours during which time germination begins. The grain is then spread out on the malting floor and turned regularly to maintain an even temperature and prevent the shoots from knitting together. During the final stage the part-germinated grain is kiln dried to stop growth and imbue it with colour and flavour. It is now *'no longer hard and steely, but crisp and crunchy like a good biscuit'* (George Luck, see below). Barley has become malt.

In the winter of 1932-3 George Luck, later to become Managing Director of St Austell Brewery, worked at a maltings in Bath as part of his training as a brewer. The process he describes here would have changed little from that in Walter's day. *'We started work at 4.30am. That meant leaving my digs*

at 4, always in pitch dark of course and usually, or so it seemed, in ice or snow. (In those days, before sufficient air conditioning, malting was only undertaken in the winter months because of the difficulty of temperature control in the summer during germination of the grain.) The first job was turning and aerating the grain on the kilns before finally unloading them. This was a hot job and a sulphurous one too from the fumes of the coke fires below. The rest of the morning was spent in turning the floors, gradually thickening the depth and then reducing it again later. This was done with large flat wooden shovels. It was hard work, very good for the development of forearm muscles, and also quite skilled, requiring a twist to throw the grain out in a wide spray, for the 'piece' as it was called had to finish completely smooth and even – no lumps or ridges. No one was allowed on the 'piece' I was given so that when George or sometimes Harold [Thompson] came around, the Foreman could truthfully report "that is all his own work".'

Turning the grain

'No longer hard and steely, but crisp and crunchy like a good biscuit. Barley has become malt'.

The Beginnings, 1851-1900

for, and knowledge of, technical advances helped to create what was even by national standards a truly modern brewery; it must have been the talk of the county. In a detailed description that appeared in the West Briton in 1870, we are told that it consisted of *'four storeys, the upper being fitted with three bins each capable of containing 100 bushels of malt, also two furnaces sufficiently large to hold 2,000 and 1,000 gallons. By a new and admirable apparatus the mashing is most successfully carried on. The next floor has two large receivers. After the beer has been boiled it is poured into these vessels in which it passes to the next flat and immediately falls on a patent refrigerator. This ingenious and useful appliance is made of a number of copper tubes and perpendicularly set, through which cold water is constantly running, as soon as the beer drops off it is then passed at its required temperature into the vats... The brewery is well supplied with spring water which is pumped by a steam engine of 3hp. The cellar is very capacious'.*

Such was the brewery's success, however, that within twenty years Walter and his son were looking for a site outside the confines of the town on which to build a new and much larger brewery.

Walter, Caroline and their children in the old Brewery House garden (now Tregarne Terrace) c.1888

A gentlemanly trade

Why did Walter Hicks choose to become a brewer? For a young man with social ambitions and a fascination with the innovations of Victorian Britain, brewing was a business with excellent prospects. Had Walter grown up at Lower Menadue he would perhaps have followed his father into farming (although the long-standing agricultural depression in Cornwall, which culminated in the failure of the potato crop in the 'Hungry Forties', might have made him think twice) but everything changed for him when his ancestral ties to the land were severed at the age of six.

The retailing of alcohol was generally considered a scurrilous occupation, particularly with the rise of the temperance movement in the nineteenth century. In 1913 the *St Austell Star* reported a heated discussion amongst members of the Urban Council over plans that had been submitted for an off-licence in Duke Street. Mr Pascoe quoted the popular moral ditty *'This is the gin shop – all glittering and gay – which helps our brothers, weak mortals, astray'*, before going on to say that *'he would rather this particular trade hid its head than make itself too prominent'*. The proposed building had, he felt, *'too much window space for the display of liquors'* (whereupon one of his more irreverent colleagues suggested that perhaps the glass could be frosted...).

However, this widespread opprobrium did not extend to commercial brewing. Indeed, as Lyn Pearson tells us in her fascinating book *British Breweries: an Architectural History,* it was overwhelmingly seen as *'a suitable occupation for gentlemen'.* As to why brewers were more socially acceptable than other Victorian industrialists, she concludes wryly that although the partial removal of the human element from practical brewing through mechanisation might have had an effect (the gentleman brewers did not have to get their hands dirty), no doubt equally telling was their capacity to make enormous profits.

Entrepreneurs were also increasingly attracted to what was an ancient trade in which scientific practice was beginning to replace some of its traditional mystique. The pace of change is reflected in the number of British patent applications concerning brewing and malting: in the 1860s there were 40 a year being received, in contrast to 27 for the entire decade of the 1830s. Walter loved his mod cons, and he had a desire to rise socially through the hot cauldron of opportunity that was Victorian industrial society; he was made to be a brewer.

Wealth from white gold

St Austell is not one of Cornwall's ancient towns. For most of its history it was a 'church-town' – just a cluster of cottages around the fine old parish church, with its remarkable carvings on the tower and outside walls – and the natural meeting place for a large rural parish. Despite a sudden growth in the eighteenth century due to a boom in tin and copper mining at Polgooth and, later, Crinnis mines nearby, it was still being described in 1842 as *'a poor town, but the parish is populous'.* In 1851 when Walter Hicks was setting up in business the population of the parish was 10,750, of which only about 4,000 lived in the town, in comparison to Truro's urban population of 16,316. St Austell however, was on the brink of a transformation.

There can be no doubt that a key factor in the meteoric success of Walter's business, along with his personal qualities as a shrewd businessman and technophile, was simply being in the right place at the right time. The second half of the nineteenth century saw the chill of dereliction and depression stealing through Cornwall, as the decline in tin and copper mining and its associated industries moved inexorably eastwards, but St Austell was protected from its harshest effects by the economic power of 'white gold'.

Back in the 1780s the Devonian chemist William Cookworthy had discovered huge reserves of china clay in Cornwall, particularly in the Hensbarrow granite moors north of St Austell. The industry developed gradually, in a localised and piecemeal fashion, until by the 1850s it was producing 65,000 tons a year and employing some 7,000 men, women and children in the St Austell area. The output then rose dramatically to more than 550,000 tons by the end of the century. This expansion was spurred on by the discovery of a multitude of uses for the curious decomposed granite far beyond its original use in the manufacture of porcelain – notably in the production of paper, paint, cosmetics and medicines.

By 1883 St Austell was considered to be *'much improved through modernising and the erection of new buildings',* and a visitor commented that *'its commerce in various branches is very considerable, and its inhabitants are in general remarked for being an industrious and thriving people'.*

Clay workers, Blackpool Pit

The new brewery, late 1890s

Chapter II
The New Brewery, 1890-1911

Much had happened to Walter Hicks in the forty years since he started work as a maltster. Step by step with the success of his business went his growth in stature as a citizen. His family had grown too; by 1890 he had ten children and was looking for somewhere larger than the Brewery House (part of Tregonissey House) to live.

His wife Emma had died of tuberculosis in 1863, having borne two daughters, and the following year he married her cousin Caroline Andrew – that 13-year-old girl from Trenance Farm who was now a handsome woman of 26. Walter and Caroline had nine children between 1865 and 1880 – two boys and seven girls (one, Mary, died in infancy) – and in due course their eldest son, also called Walter, went to work at the Brewery with his father.

Walter Hicks junior with his daughter Corona

Walter junior married Kattie Cooke in 1890, set up house at Pondhu on the western side of the town and began to raise a family. Within two years, however, he moved back into the Brewery House when his father bought the lease of one of St Austell's grandest Victorian villas: The Brake, near Trenance.

Meanwhile there were even greater changes afoot as father and son set about finding a site for their new brewery. In 1893 they found the perfect place: two open fields off Tregonissey Lane (now called Trevarthian Road), on high ground with a dramatic view over the town and beyond to the arc of empty cliffs and sparkling sea in St Austell Bay. This was still countryside in the 1890s, well outside the limits of the town;

the lane led from St Austell Church up past the steam brewery and the station above it, before heading into open country on the way to the village of Tregonissey. The two fields belonged, like so much land and property in the area, to the Sawle family of Penrice. On June 20th 1893 Walter was granted a 99-year improvement lease (the signatures witnessed, rather grandly, by *'Henry Wenman, Butler to Sir Charles Brune Graves Sawle'*). That original plot on which the brewery was built measured just *'two acres and three roods or thereabouts'*; growth and new building in the last hundred years has seen the brewery site expand to some fourteen acres today.

A mere three days after the lease was signed, the *St Austell Star* reported that: *'Mr Walter Hicks, of the St Austell Brewery, has accepted the tender of Messrs A.R. Lethbridge and Son, of Tracey Building Yard, Plymouth, for the erection of a new brewery. Messrs Inskipp and Mackenzie, of London, are the architects, and the amount of tender is between £7000 and £8000. Operations will be commenced on Monday next, and the building is to be completed in twelve months.'*

'Mr Walter Hicks, of the St Austell Brewery, has accepted the tender of Messrs A.R. Lethbridge and Son, of Tracey Building Yard, Plymouth, for the erection of a new brewery.'

Caroline in the conservatory with two of her daughters

The Brake in 1913

Hester and Elizabeth Barnes, Walter's grand-daughters, with the cockatoo, 1913

Life at The Brake

The Brake strikes an assured pose high on the precipitously steep western side of the Bodmin or Trenance valley, just over the brow of the hill from Trenance Farm. Far below, the old main road to Bodmin runs alongside the St Austell River, which rushes through dark overhanging woods and tangles of feral rhododendron.

The Brake was built in the 1860s by Thomas Martin, one of the pioneers of the china clay industry, but it had been empty for some time before Walter bought it. On the steep slopes from the house down to the river the woods were cleared to make room for the formal terraced gardens which were carved into the hillside.

Canon Hammond, in *A Cornish Parish: an account of St Austell* published in 1897, writes of The Brake that *'it is the residence of Mr Walter Hicks, and is a conspicuous object from the railway bridge as the train passes over it. Two seafaring men were one day heard to observe that "a chap with that place and three or fower pounds a week could make hisself very comfortable"!'* Having literally started on borrowed money just a few decades before, by the end of the century Walter Hicks was an extremely rich man by the standards of the day, and there is no doubt that life at The Brake was indeed comfortable if not verging on the opulent.

Walter junior's daughter Stella, who was born in 1896, has left us with the most vivid portrait of life at her grandparents' house at the turn of the century: *'I remember Granny [Caroline] as always wearing black silky dresses and lace tops with ribbons. I would sit on a footstool and she would teach me to sew. She was waited on hand and foot by her daughters – there would have been five of them at home at that time. I would be taken in to see her in the mornings*

before she was up and sit on her bed and recite the latest nursery rhyme I had learnt. After breakfast the servants would come in and join the family for prayers.

'The Brake was very attractive in those days. Looking across the valley to the Bodmin Road, the only building to be seen was the old toll cottage under the viaduct and no railway siding and houses as now. From the top of the garden one could sit and look down on a few cottages in Trenance Valley, and beyond nothing but fields and Pentewan Valley running down to the sea in the distance. Aunt Madge remembered being there when stone piers were being built on the railway viaduct to replace the old wooden ones, and saw a poor man fall to his death in the valley below. Fields on the slopes, and at the bottom of the grounds cows were kept to provide milk, cream and butter for the house.

'There was a long drive through the woods and up to the house from Bodmin Road and a tennis court at the entrance. As it was always in the shade, no grass and I imagine the surface must have been gravel! I remember the family playing 'Bumble Puppy' – a tall pole with a tennis ball attached to a long chord from the top fret and played by two people with tennis racquets. Half way up the drive, a fountain playing and goldfish in a pond. At the front door, answered of course by a parlour maid with cap streamers, one went through the conservatory – oh that lovely warm earthy smell coming up through the grating from the stoked furnace below, and the cockatoo screeching a greeting!'

The New Brewery, 1890-1911

In the mid-nineteenth century there developed a new breed of architects and engineers who specialised in the construction and fitting out of breweries. The complexities of a brewery's physical requirements demanded a concentration of expertise not usually to be found in general architectural practices. The basic challenge was how to heat, cool, move and store huge volumes of liquid in an environment where ventilation and temperature could be controlled. The key, simply in terms of the building, was to take maximum advantage of gravity and the logical way to do this, particularly in smaller breweries, was to use the traditional tower system. This was basically a refined descendant of the domestic country-house brewhouse, but on an industrial scale. At its simplest, this system has the various stages of the brewing process taking place on descending levels within the tallest part of a brewery, beginning with the initial ingredients being pumped or hoisted to the top floor and ending with a perfect pint of beer at the bottom.

By the 1870s the practice of Davison, Inskipp and Mackenzie, established thirty years earlier by Robert Davison (described by Lynn Pearson as the father of brewery architects), had grown to become one of the three specialist firms in the country. It is indicative of Walter Hicks's determination to get the best of everything that he commissioned this practice, by now called Inskipp and Mackenzie, to design his new brewery in 1893. In that same decade Inskipp and Mackenzie designed additions to some of the country's most famous breweries, including Courage's Anchor Brewery and Taylor Walker's Barley Mow Brewery in London.

Unlike some contemporaries, their work was known for being more functional than decorative. However, even the plainest Victorian industrial building has a grandeur and assurance that makes it stand out from the crowd. The most decorative and distinctive element of St Austell Brewery is the tall brick tower, a landmark for miles around, but it was not part of Inskipp and Mackenzie's design and not added until the early years of the twentieth century.

Their original 1893 building, which is still the working heart of the brewery today, is an altogether more sober affair (if such an expression can be used about a brewery). It was built to work and built to last, of good materials and a robust construction, but still has an unmistakable sense of style - a kind of austere splendour as befits its prominent position riding high on the St Austell skyline.

A kind of austere splendour as befits its prominent position riding high on the St Austell skyline.

Walter senior had retired from the day-to-day running of the business in 1890, at the age of 61, but he continued to take an active role in overseeing its development. From 1879 annual Brewers' Exhibitions – national showcases for architects, inventors and engineers – were held, initially in the Agricultural Hall in Islington, and it is not hard to imagine Walter Hicks setting off from St Austell station in his top hat to travel to London and immerse himself in all that was new in brewing. It would have been here that he discovered the work of Inskipp and Mackenzie, and

The New Brewery, 1890-1911

specialist plant manufacturers and engineers such as George Adlam & Sons and Llewellins & James, both from Bristol. As with his first venture, this new brewery was to be fitted out with the latest and the best in brewing technology.

From Adlams, Walter bought a belt-driven malt grinding mill that is still displayed at the brewery today. It was built in 1890, so if Walter bought it new then it would have started its working life down at the old brewery on Market Street before being moved up to the new site. Almost all of the original brewery plant has been modernised and replaced in the years since then, and in 2011 this beautiful machine of polished wood and brass, which used to rumble and shake like an old fairground ride on the top floor of the brewery tower, finally went into retirement.

One of the original slate fermenting vessels, made by *'Ernest Mathews & Co., Slate Back Manufacturers of London and Bristol'* probably dates from these early days. The older of the two mash tuns still in use until 2011, made by Llewellins & James, was once thought to be of this date but is now considered to have been installed when the Brewery was enlarged in 1914. The one remaining small (40-barrel) steam-heated copper is, however, part of the original Brewery plant.

Whilst there had been all this growth and change at the core of his business, what of Walter Hicks's larger estate?

As we have seen, Walter bought the leasehold of the Seven Stars at the bottom of East Hill in St Austell as early as 1863, and by 1893 he had bought a further eighteen pubs and hotels as far afield as Tavistock to the east and Gwennap to the west, closing down their brewhouses as he went. The prices of these establishments varied widely, no doubt reflecting their relative stature and

Cornish pubs in the pre-railway age

The Victorian novelist Wilkie Collins travelled through Cornwall on a walking holiday, and in his endlessly delightful account of this journey - *Rambles Beyond Railways* - describes some of the inns he encountered.

In Saltash, for instance: *'There was no mistaking the tavern. The only light on shore gleamed from the tavern window; and, judging by the criterion of noise, the whole local population seemed to be collected within the tavern walls. We opened the door; and found ourselves in a small room, filled with shrimpers, sailors, fishermen and watermen, all "looming large" through a fog of tobacco, and all chirping merrily over their cups; while the hostess sat apart on a raised seat in a corner, calm and superior amidst the hubbub...'*

And in Morvah in the far west: *'...fancy the largest of the buildings being called an inn, but making up no beds, because nobody ever stopped to sleep there: fancy in the kitchen of this inn a sickly little girl, and a middle-aged melancholy woman, the first staring despondingly on a wasting fire, the second setting before the stranger a piece of bread, three eggs, and some sour porter, corked down in an earthenware jar, as all that her larder and cellar afforded...'*

And again in Liskeard: *'Not a human being appeared in the street where this tavern of despair frowned amid congenial desolation! Nobody welcomed us at the door - the sign creaked dolefully, as the wind swung it on its rusty hinges. We walked in; and discovered a little man sitting at an empty "bar", and hiding himself, as it were, from all mortal inspection behind the full sheet of a dirty provincial newspaper... Food there was none in the house, saving a piece of corned beef, which the family had dined on, and which he proposed that we should partake of before it got quite cold. Having said thus much, he suddenly retired behind his newspaper, and spoke no word more.'*

The Commercial Inn, St Dennis, 1856

Great Western Railway at Penzance, 1904

The vital source

'Water being one of the essential materials used in brewing, it is necessary that every brewery and malting should have an abundant and constant supply. In fixing upon the site of a brewery, it is a matter of great importance that the water used for brewing should be of a kind to produce the article that is required.' (*The Brewing Industry* by Julian L. Baker, 1905).

The Brake spring

Back in 1886 Walter Hicks sent a sample of Town Water for analysis to a London firm of analytical chemists. Their report concluded that whilst it was *'a first rate town supply... for brewing purposes it is naturally not so well adapted seeing that it lacks the saline constituents so essential to the production of high class pale and bitter ales.'* They recommended that it should be artificially hardened through the addition of Burton Water Crystals which *'would bring it up very closely indeed to the Burton standard of excellence'* (the water of Burton-on-Trent being so suited to the production of light ales that it had become a national benchmark), but that for the brewing of stout and porter it was perfectly constituted and needed no additives.

We do not know if Walter took their advice or used a private well when brewing in the town, but once he had chosen a site for his new brewery he saw it as a priority to locate an independent and reliable source of water for brewing. He found it two miles up the Bodmin valley at Ruddlemoor, again on land belonging to Charles Graves Sawle who granted him the *'liberty, licence and authority to take, use and divert ... the strings and streams of water arising in or flowing from the lands...being part of the Estate of Ruddle'*, and to lay a pipeline all the way down the valley and up over the fields of Menacuddle Farm behind the Brewery. The source was only eighteen inches higher than the brewery site but that was enough to enable the water to flow by gravity without the need for pumps.

In 1906 a superior source of fresh water was found close by, issuing from an old adit (horizontal mine tunnel) on land belonging to the Martyn family of Carthew, which is now part of Wheal Martyn China

Clay Museum. A new lease was signed and the pipe was extended a few hundred yards up the valley to the adit mouth. The Carthew adit remained the Brewery's primary water supply until about forty years ago, when the expansion and deepening of the china clay pit just over the hill interrupted the supply and it began to dry up. This could have been a disaster, but since 1912 there had been a second source of water to help fill the reservoirs behind the Brewery. This spring, known at first as The Polkeys but now called The Brake from its position in the valley bottom immediately below Walter's old house (close to Menacuddle Well), now provides all the brewing water ('liquor'). Its origins are mysterious: it rises in a narrow cavern, thought to be an old mine working, which runs deep into the hillside below Bodmin Road. A limpid pool of unknown depth and constant purity, its level only dropped six inches during the drought of 1976. Modern pumps propel the water up the hill to the Brewery, and the waste water is returned to the river, after purification, just a few feet downstream from The Brake spring.

There is one more source of water used by the Brewery: the 'deep well' in the original cooper's shop which is said to have been dug by out of work miners early in the twentieth century. The particularly pure water in this well is used for general purposes today – cask washing and so forth – but in the 1920s it was also being used for brewing.

The New Brewery, 1890-1911

conditions; the Lanivet Inn was just £400 in 1893, whereas the Duke of Cornwall in Mount Charles, a large and important inn on the main road to St Austell from the east, had cost Walter £2,800 four years earlier. By 1910 the Brewery's estate had grown to 54 pubs and hotels and several more leaseholds and yearly tenancies, plus stores to aid distribution in Plymouth, Truro, St Blazey, Camborne and Penzance.

There were far fewer public houses in Cornwall by the end of the century than there had been when Walter was starting out in business, and they were mostly better regulated and run. The number of on-licences in the county dropped from 1,036 in 1864 to 650 in 1889, due to a number of factors of which the pressure of Methodism and the temperance movement was one and the shifting and loss of the mining industry another. However, the licensing authorities still had their fair share of trouble with disreputable beer shops and local dens of iniquity, and even the *bona fide* hotels and inns which catered for travellers sometimes had less than salubrious reputations. The *Royal Cornwall Gazette* in 1892 reported that two-thirds of the county's convictions for drunkenness had occurred in the parish of St Austell. The Chairman of the Annual Licensing Sessions remarked that *'It was an extraordinary thing where the people got drunk. He did not think the peculiar air of St Austell was of such a high alcoholic character as to account for it. They must have got drunk in Public Houses and he only wished it could be brought home to someone. He had private information that at the Miners Inn, Nanpean, and the Mount Charles Inn, St Austell, a great deal of drinking took place and that they wanted a good deal of looking after. As far as he was concerned he would not renew the licences of these two houses.'*

Way above all other influences, however, the extension of the national railway network to Cornwall, through the engineering skills and efforts of Isambard Kingdom Brunel, was to bring about a gradual but ultimately fundamental change in the nature of the county's

Building the Royal Albert Bridge

pubs and hotels, and was moreover to have a profound effect upon the future prosperity of Walter Hicks's Brewery. The opening of the Royal Albert Bridge over the Tamar at Saltash in 1859 heralded the era of mass tourism. It was only a trickle at first, and its true power and consequence was not to be felt until the following century, but already by the 1890s it was clear to anyone with ambitions in the victualling or hospitality business that the requirements of Cornwall's visitors needed to be addressed.

In 1910 Walter and his son took the decision to register their business as a limited company. The Memorandum of Association lists a bewildering number of *'objects for which the Company is established'*, over and above the core concerns of brewing and wine and spirits merchants, including *'any or all of the businesses of hop-merchants and growers, maltsters, maltfactors and corn merchants, bonded store keepers, wine and spirit importers and distillers, coopers and bottlers, bottlemakers, bottle shop makers, case makers, potters, manufacturers of and dealers in aerated and mineral waters and other drinks, licensed victuallers, hotel-keepers, beerhouse keepers, restaurant keepers, lodging-house keepers, ice manufacturers and merchants, tobacconists, farmers,*

Family and community

In 1910 Walter Hicks was 81 years old; a venerable and impressive figure in family photographs, with his snowy white beard and stern countenance.

He lived the life of an Edwardian gentleman, cared for by his unmarried daughters after Caroline died in 1901. His and his family's position in society and material wealth had been founded purely upon his ambition, business acumen and determination to succeed.

On the St Austell social scene, Walter had been rubbing shoulders with local landowners and the china clay 'aristocracy' since the 1870s. A.L. Rowse's description of those men whose fortune and public standing came from clay has a familiar ring to it, for it could just as well describe the founder of the Brewery: *'This was the halcyon time when the entrenched clay families made their money, heaps of it - at any rate a great deal for small people in a small place. This was the time when their villas burgeoned on the western outskirts of the town, when they prudently - they were never spendthrift - bought their first motor-cars.'*

These were the men who ran St Austell, a town which had grown so rapidly in the second half of the nineteenth century, and helped to give it its civic structure. Before the advent of the town and parish councils, the St Austell District Local Board governed the affairs of the town, employed the fire brigade and was generally responsible for town planning and improvements such as sewerage and lighting. Walter was already a member in 1869, when he was elected to serve as overseer of the parish, and by 1889 he was its Chairman. *'At a recent festive board,'* the St Austell Star reported in 1893, *'Mr Hicks humorously referred to his trade as a "poor downtrodden one" at which everybody had a kick. The "mayor" of St Austell is not without his humorous moods. This must have been one of them'.* Along with other prominent citizens, Walter was also a long-standing officer with the local Peace and Harmony Lodge of Freemasonry.

The entire Hicks family was deeply involved with the life of the parish church; Walter junior, in particular, served as churchwarden, sidesman and bellringer (he was Captain of the Tower for nearly 25 years). His daughter Stella remembered Canon Hammond being a frequent visitor to the old Brewery House, where they lived until moving up the hill to Tregarne House in 1902, and vividly recalled the recasting of the church's *fine peal of eight bells* which her father so loved to ring: *'It was fascinating living so near to watch them being brought through a window in the tower and lowered to the ground, and the same in reverse when they came back. How our local fire brigade managed while they were being recast I don't know, as the big deep toned bell was used to summon them when there was a fire. It sent shivers down one's spine to be woken up at night by the sound of its quick clang clang.'*

The New Brewery, 1890-1911

dairy-men, yeast dealers, grain sellers and driers, timber merchants, brick makers, finings manufacturers, isinglass merchants, miners and producers and merchants of china clay and china stone'.

At the first AGM of *'Walter Hicks & Company Ltd'* held on the 6th April 1910, Walter Hicks Senior was appointed Governing Director and a share capital of 10,000 shares was divided between himself and his ten children. The business was prosperous and stable; all seemed to augar well for the new company.

What should have been a comfortable and untroubled old age for Walter was, however, to be shattered just a year later. Walter junior shared his father's love of new machines and had bought his first motor cycle as early as 1904 (a 3hp Rover, registered AF145). Thereafter he had a succession of these pioneering vehicles; they were his preferred mode of transport as he travelled around the county seeing to the Brewery's scattered estate.

On the morning of 20th April 1911 he was riding down through Helston when he collided with a motor car travelling in the opposite direction and was thrown backwards off the motor cycle onto the road, fracturing his skull. The *Cornish Guardian* reported that the three gentlemen in the car *'placed Mr Hicks, who was unconscious, in their car and drove to Dr Anderson's surgery. Unfortunately there was no medical man in the town at the time, and the sufferer was then carried to a chemist's shop where first aid was rendered by PC Clarke… At first Mr Hicks was in a precarious condition, but he has since rallied somewhat and hopes are entertained for his recovery.'* The report concluded with the news that *'the eminent London specialist Sir Victor Horsely pronounced that he would recover consciousness in a few days.'* Tragically, this was not to be the case and Walter died one week later. On the day of his funeral *'one of the largest ever witnessed in the town',* the St Austell Star described how: *'About fifty employees of the St Austell Brewery preceded the hearse, and at the church gates formed a body guard. The Brewery was closed all day and business in the town was practically suspended during the internment.'*

What a devastating blow this must have been for old Walter. Quite apart from the grief of a father losing his son, there was his business to think about. He had sought to found not just a company but a dynasty, and now at the age of 82 he must have seen all that he had created suddenly look shaky and impermanent.

The provision of a secure male line to carry on the business and the family name was absolutely crucial. He had ten children, but only two were sons and now one of them, his eldest, his heir and his successor in the Brewery, was dead. His other son, George, had no interest in following his brother into the family firm. He had eight grandchildren, but again only two of them were boys and before he died he was to lose one of them, the only grandson who bore his name, in the war: Gerald Hicks, Walter junior's son, was killed at Armentières in 1915. Gerald was shot by a German sniper during a scouting mission. He was 21, and news of his promotion to Lieutenant came through shortly after his death. His Colonel wrote: *'He was one of the most gallant boys I have ever met and would go anywhere and do anything. His men adored him and his Captain could not speak too highly of him. He was intensely gallant and did not know the word "fear".'* A brother officer wrote simply: *'His men worshipped him and no words of mine can describe to you what he did for them.'*

It might have looked disastrous at the time, but with hindsight we know that Walter's dynasty did not let him down. Quite unexpectedly, it was in his remarkable eldest daughter that Walter found a worthy heir who went on to do him and his Brewery proud.

Walter and Hester in the garden of The Brake

The funeral of Walter Hicks junior

'While the muffled bells of St Austell Church tolled a solemn peal and crowds of mournful spectators with sorrowful hearts lined the streets, the body of Mr Walter Hicks junior was borne to its final resting place at St Austell Cemetery on Monday morning. The tragic death of one so universally respected lent a mournful interest to the interment, and seldom has St Austell paid such heartfelt tribute to one of its departed sons. It was an hour of general sorrow locally, and all classes alike gathered to pay their last respects to a townsman… Business houses were partially closed, and not a window was there along the entire route that was not curtained as a token of esteem and sympathy with the bereaved family.' The *Cornish Guardian*, 5th May 1911.

Tower screen in Luxulyan church, incorporating hundreds of beer bottle bottoms, given by Walter Hicks in 1912 as a memorial to his son

The Ship Inn, Mousehole

In 1901 the Ship in Mousehole became the Brewery's most distant public house when it was bought for £900. This traditional eighteenth-century pub overlooking the harbour still has its floors of scrubbed wood and huge granite flags, snugs and stained glass, low black beams and burnished panelling; its unforced charm has survived because it has been left alone. The parlour was painted by the famous Newlyn artist Stanhope Forbes (*The Green Mantleshelf*, later exhibited at the Royal Academy), and if he were to walk in there again today he would find that little had changed. The Ship was also a favoured haunt of the poet Dylan Thomas when he lived in Mousehole up on steep Raginnis Hill ('*Raginnis-is-good-for-you Hill*' as he called it) in the 1930s, but today it is best known as the home of Stargazy Pie and as the hub of festivities on Tom Bawcock's Eve.

The Ship Inn, Fowey

Walter Hicks bought the leasehold of the Ship for £500 in 1891. One of Fowey's oldest buildings, it had been the town house of the Rashleigh family. It was known as the 'Ship House' long before it became an inn because of a model of John Rashleigh's famous Elizabethan ship the *Francis* (complete with anchors, rigging, guns and men) which used to hang above the doorway on an iron chain. It is not known when the Ship ceased to be a private house, but as long ago as 1758 it was said that '*It hath been an inn of the chiefest note, in the place where situate, for a long series of time.*' A striking remnant of the old house is an oak panelled room, now a guest bedroom, carved with a figure of Elizabeth I and the date 1570.

The heroic exploits of John Rashleigh are recalled in a Victorian stained-glass window (originally from the Old Vicarage, it was bought for the Ship in 1966) depicting '*Ye shippes of Fowey Haven preparing to welcome ye Armada*'.

Rashleigh and his ship are also depicted in the dramatic scenes painted on two exterior walls in 1947 by the celebrated muralist Hans Feibusch. A German Jew who had lived in England since 1933, Feibusch is known particularly for his many church murals, and for his classical subjects painted for Clough Williams-Ellis at Portmeirion in Wales.

Hans Feibusch mural on the Ship Inn, Fowey

Images from the St Austell Brewery estate

The Central Inn, Newquay, in 1936

The London Inn, Padstow, in 2011

Mr. W. Bennets of the Queen's Head, St Stephen, in 1936

The White Hart, St Austell, in 1909

'By 1910 the Brewery's estate had grown to 54 pubs and hotels & several more leaseholds and yearly tenancies'

The Rising Sun, St Mawes, in 2004

The White Hart, St Austell, in 2009

The Ship Inn, Portloe, in 2011

Victoria Stores, Newquay, in 1936

Mr and Miss Barron of the Ship Inn, Mevagissey, in 1936

Hester Parnall

Chapter III
A Woman's Touch, 1911-1939

Immediately after his son's death, the 82-year-old Walter Hicks returned to take the helm at the Brewery, but not for long. The minutes of the directors' meeting on 22nd May 1911 read:

'I Walter Hicks do hereby appoint Hester Parnall, wife of Thomas Parnall of Belfield, St Austell, to be a Director of this Company in the place of Walter Hicks jnr now deceased'.

We can only imagine that Walter was astute enough to recognise in his daughter the qualities needed to run a business, and not to be put off by the many disadvantages of being a women in small-town Edwardian Cornwall. The Suffragette Movement might have been making the headlines in London, but its effects were barely felt in St Austell. Even today Hester would be seen as an unusually impressive figure in the business world; back then she must have been extraordinary.

Walter Hicks and Tom Parnall c.1914

Hester Parnall was 45 years old when her brother died. She had remained at home at The Brake, as one of Walter's large clutch of unmarried daughters, until the age of 39 when she married Thomas Parnall and went to live with him in some grandeur at Belfield on the Truro Road. 'Uncle Tom' was 27 years her senior; he was a kind and artistic man, an accomplished painter who loved the outdoor life and is remembered with great affection by those who knew him. Marriage to Tom gave Hester the status which her spinster sisters, however accomplished they might have been, never achieved; you would always be taken more seriously as a Mrs than a Miss.

Hester's niece Stella remembered her as a woman of strong character: *'I have heard her described as clever, witty and utterly unscrupulous. I think this last description is somewhat unfair, but one had to remember that the Aunts led very restricted lives in a small country town where there was little opportunity of fulfilling any ambition and meeting new people, or hopes of marriage or travel.'* Significantly for the future of the Brewery, Stella's son Tim Harvey considers that Hester *'had many of the characteristics and qualities of my great-grandfather'*, (whom he imagines was *'rumbustious and domineering, autocratic and impressive'*) which young Walter, *'a much quieter, gentler sort of person'*, did not possess. Clifford Hockin, who started as an office boy in the Brewery in 1926 before progressing to Company Secretary in 1963, memorably described her as:

'ruling the Company with the grace of a duchess combined with the aplomb of the successful business man'.

Hester had just five years in which to learn all that her father knew about running the Brewery. It was during this period that the brewhouse underwent some major changes to increase production. Walter Hicks's new brewery in 1893 had roughly double the capacity of his first brewery in the town; now alterations, new building and new plant installed between 1912 and 1914 doubled the capacity again, so that in less than 50 years Walter quadrupled his potential output. An extra copper room was built to house a new 100-barrel copper, replacing one of the original 40-barrel coppers, and a new enlarged fermenting room was added. However, before the work was finished the war had broken out and the effect of the consequent restricted output, escalating beer duties, reduction in beer strengths and quality, and a shortage of men and raw materials, was that this new capacity was not exploited until after 1918. By the '20s the output was close to 38,000 barrels per annum, around twice what it had been before the war.

A Woman's Touch, 1911-1939

Walter Hicks died on 4th April 1916 at the age of 87. In reporting the news of his death, the *Cornish Guardian* commented that *'a familiar figure passes out of the commercial life of the town… Mr Hicks took an active interest in the business, which under his guidance grew to such large dimensions, up to his death. He enjoyed a splendid constitution, and was in possession of all his faculties to the last. It was not until Sunday that he became seriously ill.'* Hester was made Chairman of the company on the death of her father, and under the terms of his Will she was joined on the board by her brother-in-law Reginald Garrould Barnes.

R. G. Barnes, who had married Hester's sister Mary in 1896, was the Brewery's London solicitor. He was to be a constant support to Hester in her new role, and her letters make it clear that as a matter of course she would seek his advice and respect his experience in the world of business. Her other steadfast ally was Alfred Ashton who had worked for the Brewery since 1901 and whom she made the first Manager and Secretary of the company in 1916. Their relationship was formal, as you would expect from their relative positions and the era in which they worked, but their correspondence during the times when Hester was absent from the Brewery suggests that is was also invested with mutual respect and a genuine warmth. *'It is very comforting to me to know that things are going smoothly under your direction',* she wrote to Ashton in 1924, *'and on that score I have no anxiety.'*

Hester (left) in 1922

Reginald Barnes and Mary Hicks, at The Brake on their wedding day, 1896

Despite the abilities of these two men, and the invaluable experience of brewery workers such as Mr Smallwood who took over from Mr Biscoe as Head Brewer in 1912, there is no doubt that Hester Parnall was a hands-on Chairman who involved herself with all the day-to-day aspects of running the business. Her husband Tom had died in 1915, so after her father's death the following year she moved into The Brake. In the early 1920s, however, she spent much of her time in London (before returning to Cornwall to live at Tregrehan in 1927) and a mass of correspondence between Hester and Alfred Aston during this period has survived. Thanks to the efficiency and speed of the postal and telegram services in those days, sometimes as many as three missives a day went winging their way between London and St Austell, dealing with everything from transport and brewing plant to individual workers' problems and the price of hops. These letters demonstrate Hester's demand for – and her grasp of – the details of the business at every step, as well as a financial caution that verges on meanness (contrasting, we are told, with the extravagance of her private life!). They also reveal her sharp mind, her wit, and her tendency to be forthright, opinionated and above all decisive on any matter (one memorable telegram in 1925 simply reads *'Yes. Parnall.'*)

Extracts from Walter's Will

'I bequeath all my plate and plated articles, furniture, linen, glass, china, pictures, prints, musical instruments, books… and also all my horses and carriages with their harness apparel and furniture, my motor cars with their accessories, my cows and other live and dead stock, my hothouse and greenhouse plants and other plants in pots and my stable and garden implements (but not including my small motor car nor any live or dead stock, carts, carriages, harness, implements of other chattels which at the time of my death may be used for the purpose of any trade or business in which I may be interested) unto such one or more of my daughters (except my daughter Margaret) as at my death shall not have been married….'
His unfortunate daughter Margaret *'for whom I have already otherwise provided'* was excluded from all bequests in his Will following a distressing family scandal in 1909. Poor Margaret became pregnant as a result of a love affair with a married vicar, a shattering event in those days, and was banished to Bournemouth where her child died at birth. Walter never saw her again and, as Stella later put it, *'cut her off with the proverbial shilling, though in this case it was £18,000 which was very securely tied up.'* Thereafter she lived so frugally that when she died in 1957 at the age of 84, £10,000 of interest, in addition to the original sum, was returned to her family.

Walter left Lower Menadue to his son George, but it continued to be farmed by tenants as George lived and farmed at Menacuddle just behind the Brewery. To his son-in-law R.G. Barnes, in addition to a directorship and shares in the company, he left *'my one-fourth part of or share in the business of Thomas Olver and Company China Stone Merchants'*. Hester and R.G. Barnes were appointed his Executors, and Trustees for the residue of his estate.

Memories of Hester Parnall

Clifford Hockin (worked at the Brewery 1926-1975): *'Although Hester usually visited the Brewery each morning around 11am, it was never taken for granted. All who came in contact with her, and indeed those who did not, were on their best behaviour. Before the day-to-day business was discussed, her pair of Pekingese dogs were carefully sited on the desk in the Board Room on pieces of white blotting paper laid out by the office boy [Clifford himself].'*

Tom Stephens (worked at the Brewery 1924-1973):

'The first man to spot her chauffeur-driven Daimler arriving in the yard would tap out a message of warning on the water pipes which could be heard throughout the Brewery. She once sacked a chap she caught painting with a fag in his mouth, and she sacked one of the drivers for picking up a passenger; she was a proper dragon!'

1916-17.

Walter Hicks, Esqⁿ
deceased.

Executorship and Distribution Accounts.

Miss Emma

1916				
May 18	To purchase of £400 Exchequer Bonds in your name	400		
July 20	" paid you on account	150		
Oct. 11	" One fourth Legacy duty on furniture	1	1	3
	" £3,600 Grand Trunk Railway of Canada Ordinary Stock @ 105½ transferred to you	571	5	
	" 125 British South Africa Shares @ 12/6 transferred to you	84	7	6
	" 10 £10 Shares of Walter Hicks & Co. Dᵒ @ 11 transferred to you	110		
1917 Janᵧ 9	" paid you further on account	50		
April	" £200 4½% 'B' War Stock transferred to you	200		
May	" paid you Balance of your share	74	2	3
	£	1440	16	0

Hester's letters

12th September 1925, Alfred Ashton to Hester Parnall: *'I regret to inform you that burglars broke into our Offices last night through one of the side windows between the Offices and the Bottling Store. They did not attempt to touch the safes but forced the whole of the drawers in the three bottom offices that were locked. Their total haul was about £6 which is Petty Cash received for small sales of Tobacco etc… It is the first time that a burglary has been committed here since I came 25 years ago.'*

1st January 1924, Alfred Ashton to Hester Parnall: *'Enclosed I hand you particulars of a new Foden Wagon which Jenkins of Watering is offering for £550, the price of which today is £835. Our Foden is getting pretty well worn out and I do not know what your intentions are about replacing it so I simply enclose this letter for your consideration.'*

3rd January, Alfred Ashton to Hester Parnall: *'On receipt of your telephone message today about the Foden Wagon, I saw the driver of our present Foden who told me that the one we have will go on for a year or two with little repairs…'*

5th January, Hester Parnall to Alfred Ashton: *'…it would be needless extravagance to buy another especially as the work is almost exclusively station work; prices of machines are steadily dropping and when we really need one, I daresay there will be one available.'*

Arthur Dumble and Tom Searley in the cask yard, 1942 (40 years' and 51 years' service respectively).

Brewery memories

Tom Stephens ('Tom Pip') started in the unloading shed and the wash-house in 1924, earning a 'boy's wage' of 7/6 a week, before moving to the bottling store and then to the Pop Shop, where he was paid a man's wage of £3. For three months of the year he did not get home at night until 11 or midnight, and had to be in again at 7. He had been keen to work up at the Brewery because all his friends were there, but when a vacancy came up it caused much concern to his mother and father, who were strict Wesleyans: *'They had the minister come over and they spent hours saying their prayers as to whether it was right for me to go to work at such a place of temptation. Part of the job was learning how to drink, but my excuse to mother when I got home the worse for wear was that the fumes in the Brewery had made me drunk.'*

Jack Dumble, who worked at the Brewery for 33 years, alongside his father and two of his brothers, remembered being called to be a referee at a drinking contest between Tom Searley and Arnold Walkey, at 6.45 in the morning. *'They had three gallon buckets full of beer, and Arnold did it in six minutes, on his knees like a horse.'*

'My excuse to mother when I got home the worse for wear was that the fumes in the Brewery had made me drunk.'

A Woman's Touch, 1911-1939

Hester, with Barnes and Ashton, guided the Brewery astutely through the difficult post-war years, which culminated in the economic depression of the 1930s, and under her chairmanship the company grew rapidly. The Brewery workforce expanded from 62 in 1910 to more than 80 before the outbreak of the Second World War, and in her 23 years at the helm she oversaw the acquisition of an astonishing 79 pubs and hotels.

Inevitably, with this huge expansion in the Brewery's estate throughout the county, the question of distribution became a priority. Until the 1920s, properties within a twelve-mile radius of the Brewery were supplied by horse and dray, with the railway system – then much more extensive than today – used for places further afield. In this predominantly rural county, scattered settlements and population rather than a concentrated urban base provided the Brewery's economic foundation, so horses had a crucial role to play in its early development. An L-shaped stable block closed the brewery yard to the south and east, and occupying pride of place in the middle of the yard was an enormous manure heap. Up to 20 horses lived here at any one time, their names recorded in old account books – Polly, Harold, Lion, Madam, Joey, Beauty, Kicker, Prince – and their hay, straw and mangolds supplied from Lower Menadue and Menacuddle Farms.

Early Walter Hicks bottles

The Guinness Brewery in Dublin had tried out the first steam wagons in 1897; true to form Walter Hicks was not far behind and as early as 1906 there was a steam Foden and a steam Straker covering

Brewery stables, 1890s

the short run between the Brewery and St Austell Goods Station, just down the hill. In 1912 they were joined by another Foden, and during the First World War they were used to deliver beer to the army camp on St Anthony Head at the entrance to Falmouth Harbour – a journey that took them two days. In 1928 the Great Western Railway offered to cart all goods between the station and the Brewery at 2/6 per ton, but Hester considered that *'whilst the Foden is still running it is cheaper to cart ourselves.'* At that time the annual cost of running the Foden Steam Wagon was estimated as:

Wages 2 Men . . . £301.12.0
Coal £93.12.0
Oil etc. £20.16.0
Repairs, say £12.0.0
Licence £54.0.0
Insurance £18.0.0
TOTAL . . . . . . £500.0.0 per annum

Brewery photograph

The Brewery staff in 1925. *This photograph, taken at the same time as the one of transport fleet on page 30, was the subject of an amusing discourse between Alfred Ashton and Hester Parnall in which her parsimony and his gentle insistence are well illustrated…*

AA to HP: 'I enclose herewith photographs of the Waggons and Staff at the Brewery. The largest of the staff are 5/- , the next size 3/6 and the small size 2/- each. I think they are splendid and should be pleased to hear what you think about them.'

HP to AA: 'I think the photographs are excellent. Of the staff photographs I should order three at 5/-, twelve at 3/6 and as many of the small size to give one each to the staff (excepting the Clerical Staff who will have those at 3/6).'

AA to HP: 'I have made enquiries and find that everyone without exception is anxious to have a 5/- or 3/6 size as they do not care for the small ones. They are quite agreeable to pay the difference between the cost of the small one and the one they order…They appear to look at the group as being useful as a picture in their homes.'

Mentioned by name in the book: Alfred Ashton (bottom row 8 from left). G. Smallwood (bottom row 7 from left). Bill Hockin (bottom row 2 from left). Tom Stephens (3rd row 3 from left). Tom Searley (3rd row 8 from left). Arnold Walkey (4th row 4 from left).

Brewery families

Throughout the history of St Austell Brewery, it is noticeable how the same names keep cropping up time and time again from one generation to the next: names like Hancock, Stephens, Hockin, Wescott, Cocks, Little, Henwood, Poad, Allen, Herbert, Brewer, Dumble, Searley, Walkey, Monk and Sprague. This is a true family business not just in the traditional sense – in that Walter Hicks's descendants still own and run the company – but also in that successive generations of local families have been involved in all aspects of the Brewery's work, so that over the years a tradition of family loyalty and pride in the company has developed to strengthen its very fabric and foundation.

Tom Stephens was proud that his family could notch up more than 200 years of service to the Brewery, with a total of fourteen members of the family having worked there since he started in 1924. He remembered being so careful not to show favouritism to his son that:

*'I went too far the other way.
He said I was the worst boss ever!'*

Brewery memories

Clifford Hockin: *'Fred Burchall was the chief horse-man, a seven day a week job, on call 24 hours a day. For this service he enjoyed rent-free accommodation of the cottage adjoining the stables. He lost this job and cottage when it became known that for two evenings a week he was running a Hoop-la Stall in the Market House. He then drove the steam Foden for a time but lost this job too as he never could stop the Foden without shouting 'Whoa! Whoa there!' in panic at the top of his voice.'*

In 1924 the Brewery bought a new boiler, the old one having been condemned by the Boiler Insurance Co., and Clifford Hockin remembers the Foden being used to haul it up the hill from the railway station: *'This was an exciting event and attracted much interest throughout the journey. The boiler was both loaded on to the new five-ton Leyland petrol lorry and on to the Foden to distribute the weight. The Foden was to lead and the Leyland to follow, but in reverse gear. All went well, very slowly, until the steep entrance to the Brewery was reached, when the front wheels of the Foden rose into the air like a prancing horse.'*

The following letter from Alfred Ashton to Hester Parnall makes it clear that the boiler completed its journey successfully, as well as revealing something of the fondness in their working relationship: *'I regret very much to hear that your are unwell and not able to come down. I shall feel quite lost without you at the Meeting tomorrow but after all I do not consider it wise for you to run any risks whatever. You can rest assured that all matters will be carried through in proper order by Mr Barnes and myself…I am pleased to say that everything is alright at the Brewery and the Fires of the New Boiler were lit by Miss Carrie* [Hester's sister Caroline Hicks] *and Mr Barnes this morning.'*

> *"All went well, very slowly, until the steep entrance to the Brewery was reached, when the front wheels of the Foden rose into the air like a prancing horse."*

A Woman's Touch, 1911-1939

Before long the first petrol lorries joined the horses and the steamers – initially two Federals, two Maxwells and a Thornycroft – but the horses' days were numbered. The minutes of the directors' meeting on 3rd July 1923 recorded the resolution *'to purchase a two-ton and a five-or six-ton Leyland lorry. Horses to be disposed of as soon as big lorry is delivered'*. However, horses continued to be used elsewhere in the county to deliver from certain stations to the outlying pubs. Ashton wrote to Hester Parnall in May 1925 that: *'Maunder has appealed to me for additional help for his delivery of goods at Newquay…The season is fast approaching and we have nothing there at present but a worn out old horse and wagon and every appearance of having a very busy time.'* In 1930 it was reported from Penzance *'that at the present we are hiring transport owing to the horse having died…'*

As the Brewery expanded its estate and updated its transport system, so much of Hester's and R. G. Barnes's attention was also given to modernising some of the brewing plant which new advances, particularly in bottling and refrigeration, had rendered obsolete. Crown corks, now the usual method of sealing bottles, were introduced during this period; an American invention

Brewery dray delivering in St Ives, 1900

A Woman's Touch, 1911-1939

patented in 1892, they revolutionised the production of bottled beers, in terms of both the speed of the bottling and the efficiency of the seal. The Brewery bought its first crown corking machine second-hand for £40 in 1927 from the Friary Brewery in Guildford.

Prior to this, the bottles were sealed with either corks (stoppers, as opposed to driven corks, at this stage), screws or 'cods'. The oldest cod bottles were pear-shaped and had a glass marble inside which, combined with a rubber ring at the mouth, acted as a seal when the bottles were filled under pressure. In its Mineral Waters Department (the 'Pop Shop'), which had been an essential part of Walter Hicks's business from the earliest days, the Brewery produced prize-winning lemonade, ginger beer, mineral water and soda water. In the early days most of the minerals were bottled in cods, but soda water was also produced in syphons, whilst the celebrated Hicks's Ginger Beer came in half-pint corked and wired stone bottles know as 'Stonegingers'.

Two of the most significant changes in the Brewery's history came in 1934. In October, after lengthy and complex negotiations, the Company bought Christopher Ellis & Son's Steam Brewery at

Sketch by R. G. Barnes of possible crown cork design, included in letter

Hayle, together with its estate of 30 licensed premises, for £50,000. In the same year the name of the Company was changed to *'St Austell Brewery Co. Ltd'*. This was not such a surprising move as for many years it had been referred to as 'the St Austell Brewery' both informally, to identify the location of Walter Hicks's Brewery, and formally – for instance on the livery of the transport fleet (see the photograph below). R. G. Barnes wrote to A.S.B. Payne in June 1934: *Mrs Parnall and I are seriously considering the change of the name of the Company from Walter Hicks & Co. Ltd to St Austell Brewery Co. Ltd. This could conveniently be done at the present time when various other changes in the constitution of the Company are contemplated. Do you see any objection to the change? I am advising you of this beforehand so that you may keep down the stock labels, crown corks, invoices, letter paper etc. to the minimum dimensions.'*

The transport fleet in 1925, housed in the old stables

Ellis Brewery labels

The purchase of the venerable Ellis Brewery brought about a significant expansion of the business in the west of the county where all of its houses were located. The Ellis family had been brewing in Hayle since 1815, but the handsome buildings in use in the 1930s dated from 1873. Unusually extensive records of this once thriving company have survived; Paul Stephens, who has an exhaustive knowledge of Ellis history, describes how in its early days *'beer, wine and spirits would seem to have been almost less important than general trading and merchandising…At various times the brewery sold such diverse items as wheat, barley, apples, pigs, pipes, tobacco, reeds, clover, nails, white sugar, salt, malt and cheese.'*

Early Walter Hicks bottles, including Stonegingers

The Lugger Inn, Polruan

This traditional quayside fisherman's pub had been owned and run by successive generations of the Hicks family (no relation, but a long-standing Polruan family) for nearly a century when it came up for auction in 1937. By this time, Hester's health was failing and her old allies Alfred Ashton and R.G. Barnes had both died. In Ashton's place as Manager and Secretary there was A.S.B. Payne, who had proved a worthy and dependable successor. Payne wrote to Hester in November 1937 that *'On Wednesday I went to Polruan to look at the Lugger Hotel. It is quite a nice little house and beautifully kept, but it is like all these old fashioned houses and has a lot of small rooms and not any large ones.'*

At the auction the Brewery was outbid by an individual who paid £4,415. It was, in Payne's view, *'an absurd price'*, but he was at least relieved that the pub had not been bought by a rival brewery such as Devenish or Redruth because he had established that the buyer would be likely to have the Brewery supply it as a free house. However, in the minutes of the Directors' meeting held in January 1938 it was reported that *'the purchaser subsequently was unable to complete and offered the house to the Company and the property was purchased for £3,800 on January 5th'*.

The St Kew Inn

In 1922 Hester Parnall bought the St Kew Inn, today one of the Brewery's best-loved rural pubs, as one of eight properties owned by the business of A. Coombes & Son of Wadebridge. Coombes were described as *'Wine and Spirit Merchants, Mineral Water Manufacturer, Hop Merchant, Maltsters and Cigar Merchants'*, and for an outlay of just £6,500 the Brewery acquired some notable houses – including the Golden Lion in Port Issac and the Earl of St Vincent in Egloshayle – along with the Eddystone Road headquarters of the business itself.

The beautifully-proportioned Georgian building, set close by the church in the classic Cornish churchtown of St Kew, started out as a private house but has been the St Kew Inn since the early nineteenth century. What is now the public bar was once the hall-kitchen of that house; the slate flagstones and black settles, the meat hooks hanging from the ceiling, and the vast fireplace with a cast-iron expanding grate and logs stacked on either side are reminders of the pub's former life.

A Woman's Touch, 1911-1939

He also recounts the story of a rhyme, which was supposedly to be found carved on a lintel in the Dolcoath Mine count house.

'If you don't drink Ellis' beer, you don't work here!'

Christopher Ellis

Therein, you could say, lay the source of this brewery's strength but also its ultimate downfall. The fortunes of the Ellis Brewery were shackled to those of the mines, the foundries and the shipyards of West Cornwall, an area whose economy had already been devastated and whose population decimated long before the final blow of the worldwide economic depression of the 1930s. Brewing ceased in 1934 and the Hayle brewery became St Austell Brewery's main depot in the west, until it closed in 2006. Christopher Ellis junior, known as Chrissie, joined the Board of St Austell Brewery as a salaried director, and preferential shares were issued to members of the Ellis family.

In the year 2000 Ellis beer was drunk again in Hayle for the first time in 66 years. St Austell's Head Brewer Roger Ryman brewed a special one-off ale from an Ellis recipe of 1872 discovered by Paul Stephens and took it to CAMRA's national festival in London; fittingly, it was also available at the Cornish Arms in Hayle, just across the road from the old brewery.

A year after the purchase of the Ellis Brewery, in which he had played such a key legal role, R.G. Barnes died aged 66; he had retired from Kent to Cornwall two years earlier and taken a lease on Trenarren House, but was given tragically little time to enjoy it. He was replaced on the Board by his son Egbert Barnes, the only surviving grandson of Walter Hicks.

In 1927 Hester had taken a lease on Tregrehan, the ancestral home of the Carlyon family, and here at last she found herself in a place that was grand enough to suit her. She lived at Tregrehan on and off (interspersed with sojourns in London and Kent) until 1936 and was able to indulge her love of gardening in a long-established and historically important ornamental landscape. The garden at Tregrehan dates from the 1840s and later and is considered by many to have the finest collection of exotic trees and shrubs in Cornwall.

Hester entertained some illustrious visitors here, most notably the Prince of Wales (later Edward VIII) and Mrs Simpson during one of their trips to Cornwall when they used to stay at the nearby Carlyon Bay Hotel (then called the St Austell Bay Hotel). Hester's great-nephew Tim Harvey recalls:

'I was terrified of Aunt Hester's butler at Tregrehan, and the fact that she had one! She was very keen on gardening, as was the Prince of Wales, and I think that's how she met him – she managed to inveigle him to come and see the gardens at Tregrehan and it became a great social feather in her cap.'

Birth of a brand

In the late 1920s the Brewery's stock draught brews were XX, XXX, XXXX (bottled as Brown Willy Ale, named after Cornwall's highest hill), PA, BB (bottled as Light Ale) and IPA (India Pale Ale), but the Head Brewer Mr Smallwood was looking to develop a new stronger bottled beer to compete with popular pale ales produced by Bass and Worthington. The following extracts from letters chart the progress of this new product whose name was to become a Brewery standard:

16th December 1927, Mr Gillett (Manager and Secretary 1927-30) to R. G. Barnes: *'I have been amusing myself trying to get out a new label for the higher gravity Beer we intend to put before the Trade. There is a great deal in the name and the difficulty is to get one "snappy" enough to "catch on". Mrs Parnall rather liked the name "Duchy". Should we be sailing too near the wind, as regards the triangle as I have shown it, which is, you know, Bass's trade mark? As an alternative to this, how would it be to substitute a map of Cornwall and on it mark in the Branches?'*

30th December, W. J. Cummins (printer) to the Brewery: *'I am enclosing herewith a sketch of your Duchy Ale label. The colours are red and black to match your Crown Cork, but you could, if you desired, have the words "The Brewery, St Austell" in green.'*

4th January 1928, R. G. Barnes to Mr Gillett: *'I agree with Mrs Parnall in preferring the label marked with the red cross at the back, but I think this label could be considerably improved by a better drawing of the county of Cornwall. I have roughly traced on the covering paper the outline of Cornwall from an atlas which will shew you how much the draughtsman is out in getting the proper outline…'*

12th January, R. G. Barnes to Mr Gillett: *'The Controller of Trade Marks is not in favour of my proposal to register "Duchy" as our trade mark. Under the Act he is not allowed to register as a trade mark a word "according to its ordinary signification a geographical name". At any rate, if a formal application is turned down for us, it cannot be granted for anyone else, and I cannot think that if we start using the mark any decent brewer would imitate it. Thanks to Mr Smallwood we have got hold of a good name. The next thing is to produce a beer to match it, which is Mr Smallwood's job.'*

13th January, Mr Gillett to R. G. Barnes: *'I suggested to Mrs Parnall yesterday that it might be worth while to have a couple of gross or so of Show cards, having in the centre an enlarged copy of our new label and printed on it, say, "Try our Duchy Ale. 6d per bottle" or something of that sort, I suggest that it should be hung in the Bars of Houses to draw customers' attention that there was something new about… I am putting in the first brew on Monday week, this should be ready for bottling about the time we shall probably receive the labels etc.'*

11th February, R. G. Barnes to Mr Gillett: *'Mrs Parnall and I have been discussing the Salasigns. We think for the Maxwells and the Durrant a smaller sign with DUCHY ALE only will be sufficient. For the larger wagons DRINK DUCHY ALE with DUCHY in silver.'*

14th February, Mr Gillett to R. G. Barnes: *'I have today sent to you per Passenger Train a case containing one dozen bottles of Duchy Ale. I think the beer will improve after being another ten days in cask, to me it seems at present somewhat green, but there is a nice hop palate. I asked them to enclose some Crown Cork openers in the case, as you may not have any.'*

6th March, Mr Smallwood to R. G. Barnes: *'You will be pleased to hear that I think Duchy Ale is going well, everyone is sending in repeat orders. We are racking another Brew tomorrow and on Friday are brewing again. A "gentleman" was seen to be making tracks for home (Mount Charles) a few evenings ago; he was not capable of demonstrating Euclid's definition of a straight line, and when he wobbled there were, I understand, cries of "Up Duchy!" "Up Duchy!"'*

It was a good name, and it continued to be used for many decades. A new bottled Duchy was introduced (as 'Royal Duchy' at first) in 1954, and the name was later transferred to the award-winning keg bitter originally called Extra. Duchy finally ceased production in February 2009.

The Yacht Inn, Penzance

The designs of the pool and the Yacht were strongly influenced by the Modernist movement in European architecture; they are both important historic structures and they bring to the Penzance seafront the unmistakeable *élan* of those pre-war years.

The Yacht, 1936, before rebuilding

The Yacht was one of the 30 houses that came to the Brewery in 1934 with the purchase of the Ellis Brewery. Originally called the Mariner's Arms (*'and remembered as such by me'*, wrote Chrissie Ellis in 1929), it cost £1500 and was in a somewhat run-down state by that time, with only a beer-shop licence rather than a full one. In 1936 the Brewery appointed the Penzance architect Mr Drewitt, of Cowell, Drewitt and Wheatly, to rebuild the Yacht in a style to complement the nearby Jubilee Bathing Pool on the Promenade which had been opened in 1935. This fabulous open-air tidal lido, restored in 1990 and now a listed structure, was designed by Frank Latham, the Penzance Borough Engineer. It is memorably described by Roger Deakin in his wonderful book *Waterlog*:

The new Yacht in 1938

'With its dramatic ocean-liner decks, stainless-steel fittings, steps and tubular railings, the Jubilee Pool is highly theatrical…It is pure 1930s in its exuberant, extravagant use of concrete and in the flowing lines of its romantic, impractical shape.'

Aerial view of Penzance seafront, showing the Jubilee Pool and the Yacht

A Woman's Touch, 1911-1939

Cecil Brewer, who worked at the Brewery from 1927 to 1975, remembers a grand fête held at Tregrehan in honour of the Prime Minister Stanley Baldwin. Hester, a lifelong Conservative supporter, had the Brewery shut down for the day so that everyone could (and had to!) attend the fête.

It was the first time that a Prime Minister had visited Cornwall during his tenure of office, and an estimated 20,000 people (and 800 motor vehicles) turned up at Tregrehan on that June day in 1927 to hear him speak. The *Cornish Guardian* described in detail the *'gigantic picnic'* held in the park, with stalls, roundabouts, trick-cycling, wrestling tournaments, athletic sports, tug-of-war competitions and clay target shooting. Three silver bands led the crowd in community singing (including 'Trelawny') and Hester Parnall judged the *'best decorated bicycle'* competition.

"What a picture! A wonderful sight"

ejaculated the Prime Minister as he stepped on the gaily-beflagged platform in the lovely grounds of Tregrehan and waved toward the green slope on which a great crowd cheered and waved flags and handkerchiefs in greeting. No more suitable spot for a great Cornish conservative demonstration could have been chosen than the residence of Mrs T. R. Parnall.' The *Cornish Guardian*.

In addition to her ever-present Pekingeses, Hester kept a Minah bird at Tregrehan which constantly used to repeat the words *'kiss me nice!'* Apparently it had learned the phrase from Hester's chauffeur who used to say it to the parlourmaids.

Hester Parnall died on 20th April 1939 at the age of 73. She had been troubled by painful ailments in her last years of life, including persistent rheumatism, and broke her hip in June 1938 (her immobility thereafter prevented her from living at

Point Neptune in Fowey, which she had bought after leaving Tregrehan), but it seems that her fundamental health was good and her death took everyone by surprise. As late as 7th April she was still firmly in the saddle, writing briskly to Mr Payne to advise against buying German-made glass-lined tanks: *'I roused Mr Barnes this morning from his slumbers to give him my opinion about the tanks and he agrees with me that they should not be German.'*

Chrissie Ellis's letter of condolence to Egbert Barnes on hearing of her death serves as a heartfelt valediction to this remarkable woman: *'I don't know how to express my sorrow at the sad death of Mrs Parnall. I little thought when we met in St Austell a short time since that it was for the last time, she was so bright and cheerful then. It seems so hard after all she has gone through since last June and the brave way in which she faced it all that her good and useful life should terminate so abruptly. Please accept from my family and myself the deepest sympathy with you all in your sad loss.'*

Tregrehan in 1928

Left to right: Egbert Barnes, Kenneth Moore and George Luck

Chapter IV
Steady Hands, 1939-1979

Hester Parnall was succeeded as Chairman of the Brewery by Egbert Barnes; 1939 was to prove to be quite a year for this 41-year-old lawyer, who had had less than four years on the Board since his father died and now suddenly found himself in the hot seat.

It was clear from the start, however, that Egbert was more than a match for the job; he was able to combine his father's thoroughgoing knowledge with a boundless enthusiasm for and loyalty to the Brewery and a delightfully irreverent and youthful sense of humour. In a letter of June 1938, A.S.B. Payne had cause to remind Egbert gently that he had not responded to Payne's earlier request to use the company seal on an excise entry. Egbert replied immediately, in the form of a telegram sent from Lords Cricket Ground: *'YES USE SEAL. AUSTRALIA 315 TO WIN'.* His forty years at the helm were to be ones of unforeseen challenge and change; that the Brewery not only survived but flourished during this time, and that everyone who remembers him does so with enormous respect and affection, are testimony to the character of this man.

Two months after Hester's unexpected death, the Brewery was to face another crisis when a serious fire broke out in the garages in the yard, supposedly caused by a Thornycroft lorry overheating. Cecil Brewer recalls that it was the eve of the Royal Cornwall Show and all the lorries were loaded up with beer ready to be taken to the show the following morning. It was a windy evening and before long the entire L-shaped range of buildings enclosing the yard to the south and east was aflame; here were housed the garages (formerly the stables), the carpentry and paint shops, the fitters' shop, and highly inflammable paint store and timber store, along with the gatekeeper's cottage where Bill Burt and his family lived. The *Cornish Guardian* reported that: *'In the earlier stages of the fire, the bursting of the petrol tanks and the explosion of bottles had been reminiscent of the early stages of a bombardment in warfare and the flames were too fierce to approach to within 50 feet.'*

Despite this, a handful of Brewery employees managed to rescue furniture, as well as one lorry, a light van and two private cars. They were helped by cricketers who abandoned the game they had been playing nearby; Clifford Hockin recalled that *'amid cheers from*

The stables on fire 12th June 1939

The same view the following day

Steady Hands, 1939-1979

the onlookers, first the cricketers and then the St Austell Boy Scouts arrived, formed a chain and helped remove the furniture from the cottage.' The town's new fire engine *Ruby* was on hand; it was her first outing but not a particularly auspicious one since the water pressure in the hydrants was so low that all that emerged from the hose was an ineffectual trickle which ran down the arm of fireman George Thomas. Eventually, water from the reservoirs up behind the Brewery was used to get the fire under control.

Many old Brewery records, which had been stored in boxes in the upstairs rooms, were lost in the fire along with the buildings themselves (later partially rebuilt at a cost of £795) and four new Bedford lorries. However the show had to go on, and four days later A.S.B. Payne was writing to Egbert Barnes in stalwart tones:

'In spite of all our troubles this week, trade is up 34 Barrels, which is quite satisfactory.'

Less than five months after he had taken over as Chairman, Egbert had to face a very different crisis with the outbreak of war. Two days after Britain had declared war on Germany, Egbert wrote to A.S.B. Payne, whom he had promoted from Manager and Secretary to be the Brewery's first Managing Director: *'It's a great relief to my mind to know I have you in charge and in authority at the Brewery, and if any further justification of the appointment I was so glad to make as soon as I took over was needed – which it isn't – we certainly have it now. Keep me in touch as much as you can. It helps and cheers me to know how things are. Our maxim must be to go slow and cut out all frills till we see how things stand.'*

In July 1939 Egbert had made his priorities as Chairman of the Brewery quite clear in a written declaration of his thoughts and aims, which today might be described as his mission statement. Prophetically subtitled *'If Hitler lets us!'*, the list opens with: *'Our first and constant aim must be directed to raising wages to a decent minimum'*. Further on, he suggests the idea of *'some sort of Brewery Council with the powers and duties laid down in the opening chapters of the Rowntrees book* The Human Factor in Business, *as far as it is applicable to a small business',* and muses that *'I shouldn't be surprised if everyone in the Brewery could not point out some small thing which, if altered, would improve his work or comfort. It may be no more than a window that rattles or a lack of light in some corner…'* This, then, was a very different creature from his predecessor; for Egbert Barnes the welfare of the workforce and the welfare of the company were inextricably linked, and his natural sense of justice and fair play meant that he wanted the best possible conditions for everyone.

He had nailed his colours to the mast early on, whilst his aunt was still Chairman, by encouraging her to introduce a company pension scheme in 1938, some time before most other comparable businesses had thought of such a thing. Based on a very small percentage of the weekly wage, plus the company's contribution, it produced an annual pension for each year of service plus free life insurance and disablement benefit during the year. Cecil Brewer remembers that the Brewery management took time and care to clarify this unfamiliar proposal: *'The pension scheme, it was Mr Barnes's idea and when they mooted it we used to go up in the bottling store and the whole brewery was there and somebody explained it to us. I think we had two or three meetings and you could pop questions if you wanted. Wages were very low, and they said you had to take so much a week out; but eventually we voted to have it – good thing too.'*

For the first six years of Egbert's Chairmanship, however, it was the war that dictated the course of Brewery business. The company had to learn how to operate with a restricted workforce and to adapt to shortages in raw materials and fuel and the loss, through

Memories of Egbert

Clifford Hockin: '*A great leader, he was also an intensely human man with an infectious and almost schoolboy enthusiasm. "Crikey" and "Golly" were often among his exclamations of surprise or delight together with an acute yet splendidly broad sense of humour. He was always eager for advice and opinions yet when it came to the put-to he unhesitatingly accepted the responsibility for the ultimate decision. One of his senior staff once said of him "When things go right it is to us he gives the credit and when they go wrong he is the one who takes the blame".*'

'*Mr Barnes? He was a gentleman.*' Cecil Brewer.

Egbert's letters

28th September 1937, Egbert Barnes to A.S.B. Payne on receiving the routine monthly figures:

'*August – "quite good"? August damn well magnificent! My heartiest congratulations to you and all concerned.*'

February 1943, Egbert Barnes to Claude Aylwin on the subject of interviewing prospective tenants for one of the Brewery's hotels: '*I was very favourably impressed by them. He is quite presentable; she must have been very nice looking; the daughter, a grass widow with a husband in the RAF, is very nice looking. (I imagine she was brought up with a view to impressing susceptible chairmen). They have no hotel experience at all…Mrs W. was emphatically confident that she could manage the catering and hotel side, and daughter, fixing her soulful eyes upon me and doing a bit of a flutter of the eyelids, said that her mother was a most competent person…Altogether I feel you will think that I am **not** a competent person to interview prospective hoteliers…*'

The Swastika stoppers

One bizarre effect of the rise of the Nazi party in Germany in the 1930s was that St Austell Brewery had to have all its old bottle tops (screw stoppers) drilled out or ground down to erase the image of a swastika with which they were stamped as a trade mark.

When and why the Brewery adopted this symbol is not known, but the swastika had been used throughout history and by almost every culture in the world as a common decorative motif. Its meaning varied slightly from country to country and from faith to faith, but the origin of the word is from the Sanskrit for 'conducive to well being', and it was generally used as a token of good luck. However, ancient forms of the symbol tended to have it resting flat and with the arms facing anti-clockwise, whereas the swastika adopted by the German Nazi Party faced clockwise at a 45-degree angle. Curiously, the Brewery swastika also faced clockwise, as can be seen from the stoppers that survived.

The White Hart, St Austell

The White Hart had been St Austell's foremost inn for centuries, situated at first in Fore Street (where it was described by a traveller in 1799 as *'the best we had seen in Cornwall'*) before moving to its present grander premises in the early nineteenth century. Unlike so many houses that still bear the name, this is an inn in the proper sense of the word in that it provides accommodation. The splendid building started life as a town house for Charles Rashleigh, who was responsible for the development of the port at Charlestown. At that time it was two-storied, but the Brewery added the top storey in 1925, having bought the White Hart in 1911 for £5,000. Despite being the classiest establishment that St Austell had to offer, it still at that time had a notorious tap room which, the *St Austell Star* reported in 1912, *'was a habitual resort of prostitutes'*.

The famous French wallpaper dating from *c.*1800, which used to adorn the dining-room with Italian landscape scenes, was given by the Brewery to the British Museum in 1935. Hester Parnall wrote to A.S.B. Payne on the 1st December: *'I hope the B. Museum men have had some measure of success getting the paper off at the W. Hart. I am amazed at the interest it has caused. I daresay the Public think we have received a mighty sum for it, instead of being the other way round!'*

Wallpaper in the White Hart dining-room

During the war the White Hart took on a new role that was to continue for many successful years, initiated by Egbert Barnes who had a particular interest in contemporary British art. In the summer of 1944 he organised, in conjunction with Borlase Smart and the St Ives Society of Artists, the first of many exhibitions of paintings at the White Hart. Over the years since then some of the best-known names in modern art have hung their works here, including Peter Lanyon, Augustus John, Paul Nash and Ben Nicholson. Extracts from the Foreword he wrote for that first show tell us

much about Egbert's character and guiding principles: *'This Exhibition of Pictures is an experiment, and this is why it is being made…I determined some ten years ago to make an effort to understand what the Artist of the present day was doing. I gave myself six months and if at the end of that time I could make nothing of him, I said I would give it up. I never have given it up. I was often mystified: I am often still mystified. But I have got a great deal of pleasure…Now how, even if he wants to, can a man follow the work of Contemporary Painters? It involves going round the small commercial galleries and seeing what is on, but they only exist in London. They are not much good to us in Cornwall. This, then, is an attempt to provide in St Austell something of the same facilities that exist in London, but with this difference: these pictures are priced by the Artists and we charge neither commission nor expenses for the Exhibition. If they are sold, purchasers can take them away on payment. For this reason the pictures will be continually changing (or so we hope)… We hope particularly that the Art Masters of any of our local schools will bring their students to see the pictures…'.*

In 1963 Egbert was amused to recall *'my colleagues' pained surprise'* when in 1946 he had brought two Ben Nicholson paintings for the Brewery for £50 and £30. Seventeen years later they were sold at Sotheby's for £2,350 and the proceeds paid for the entire refurbishment of the White Hart!

Recently the White Hart has had another important role to play in the life of the Brewery, and in the regeneration of St Austell, since its transformation into an award-winning training centre of excellence for the licensed trade and the wider hospitality business.

requisition, of most of its transport fleet. Brewing was classified as an essential food industry; although excise duty was high, beer was not rationed and in fact breweries were encouraged to increase production in order to supply the troops and to maintain morale on the home front.

The sudden death of A.S.B. Payne in July 1942 was a particular blow; the calm expertise which he brought both to management and then to the Board had been enormously appreciated by Egbert in his difficult first years. Kenneth Moore, from the company's firm of auditors, had joined the Board in 1939 as a non-executive director, but now Egbert was left with an urgent need for a good reliable Managing Director at a time when manpower was in short supply. Soon after Payne's death he wrote this characteristically straightforward letter to Claude Aylwin, a man whom he had never met but who had been suggested to Kenneth Moore by a mutual acquaintance: *'You won't know me from Adam, nor will the signature at the foot of this leave you much wiser so I'll introduce myself as*

soon as possible. I am the Chairman of a small family brewery – the St Austell Brewery Co. – in Cornwall. Our Managing Director, one A.S.B. Payne, an awfully good chap, has died suddenly and we are looking for a successor… The object of this letter is to know if you would like to consider the job. I must tell you a little more about the company. Capital £250,000, the ordinary shares (£200,000) being all held by my family. No debentures. Barrelage about 25,000 a year. Profits round about the £40,000 mark. We've got a jolly good staff and a clever brewer in one Smallwood, though he's nearer 70 than 65, alas. I think I can say it's a thoroughly clean little business and I am sure that there are no skeletons in any of its cupboards. Payne used to run the show entirely and I had absolute confidence in him. I live in Wiltshire; we kept in touch mostly by telephone and I used to go down once a month or so to look around…'

Much to Egbert's relief, Aylwin took the job and, with the aid of the Company Secretary Mr Giles, ran the brewery efficiently through the remaining war years. In 1943 the Brewery entered into a rare alliance with its chief rival – the

The Ship Inn, Pentewan, one of the houses previously owned by the Treluswell Brewery

Redruth Brewery – to buy the Treluswell Brewery Company and its twelve tied houses. Brewing had ceased on Treluswell Hill, just outside Penryn, and the old brewery buildings were disposed of but St Austell was able to add six houses to its estate for a total of £15,000. Four more houses were bought during the war, three of which were important old coaching inns on main roads through the county: the Victoria at Roche, the London Inn at Summercourt and the Victoria at Threemilestone.

Left to right: Jack Herbert, A.S.B. Payne and Kenneth Moore in 1935

Steady Hands, 1939-1979

The Brewery by now had a large and scattered estate which, due to the restrictions of wartime, was in a poor state of repair. As early as 1942 Egbert was thinking ahead, despite the uncertain outcome of the conflict. He ordered a survey of all the houses, working from Bude westwards:

'So that a programme of necessary repairs and desirable improvements and where necessary rebuilding might be drawn up ready to put into operation after the war.'

As the war drew to a close, the Board repeatedly voiced its concern about the visual and structural dilapidation of its houses and made it clear that this was to be the Brewery's post-war priority.

Plans were in place, but the Brewery's long-term programme of improvement and modernisation did not really get into gear until the advent of a new Managing Director who joined the company in 1946, succeeding Claude Aylwin on his retirement in the following year. The ensuing partnership between George Luck and Egbert Barnes was an extraordinary combination of longevity, commitment and friendship, and it gave the Brewery the strength and stability to survive the choppy waters of that unknown post-war world. In his memoirs, written for his children after retirement, George recalled how it all began: *'Egbert Barnes and I met for the first time in our long association at 9 o'clock on a Saturday morning in early August on Paddington Station. Before long he asked me what my plans were for the rest of the morning. "Nothing at all important" I replied, "but I had been hoping to go down to my parents in Sussex for the weekend which would mean I would be getting a train from Waterloo later on." "Capital!" exclaimed Egbert. "I want to got to Waterloo too; let's walk there shall*

we?" And so we did, talking non-stop the whole way. It is fair to say that we got on well together from the first moment and fortunately continued to do so for the next 33 years until we both retired in 1979.' George found out later that he had been something of a late entrant; there had been 200 applicants for the job (advertised as *'General Manager, with prospects of promotion to Managing Director'),* and Egbert had actually been on his way to Waterloo to offer the job to someone else, so that was a crucial walk they took on that Saturday morning.

George had trained as a brewer before the war, and since leaving the army had been working as an Outside Manager for Taylor Walker & Co. at their Barley Mow Brewery in Limehouse (a splendid building which, like St Austell, was designed by Inskipp and Mackenzie; it was demolished in the 1960s). At 32 some thought him too young and inexperienced for management, his career having been rudely interrupted by six years distinguished service overseas, but they were won round by Egbert's instinct that he was the right man for the job. On George's first visit to the Brewery, Egbert was keen that he should have a chance to look around before making a final decision: *'We were met at St Austell station by Howard Henwood, the first St Austell Brewery man I ever met, and the first brewery pub I saw was the Cornish Arms (or Fifteen Balls as it was known) from the window of the train at Par. It looked rather drab but I was at once impressed by the distinction and simplicity of the gold and black lettering of the sign. The first pub I visited was the Crown Inn at St Ewe. Our tenant there was a hard-bitten, tough and forthright Cornishman and I remember his words when I was introduced as the prospective new manager. "Well b****r!" he said to Egbert. "He's a cheerful looking b****r anyway, which is more than what the other b****r is, b****r 'ee".'*

George's mention of the characteristic gold and black lettering touches upon a significant aspect of the Brewery's history. When he and Egbert began the mammoth task of redecorating and upgrading all the public houses, the one thing they did

Memories of George Luck

Doing a proper job

'He used to go around the Brewery every Friday afternoon and have a chat with everyone, see everyone, called everyone by their Christian names. He was different; you could talk to him.' **Cecil Brewer**

Clifford Hockin: 'He would call regular meetings of the whole Brewery to hear everyone's views, and so that everyone knew what was happening. When he walked round on Friday afternoons he knew everyone and had a word for them all; he thought about people and remembered everything about them.'

Tim Harvey: 'George had the foresight to see how the future was going to go, and he had the biggest influence on the Brewery expanding on the wines and hotels side. He'd been a traditional brewer before the war, but he saw that the company needed to embrace all sorts of other skills and ideas rather than just brewing gallons and gallons of beer. He was a great traditionalist in lots of ways, but he was also very forward looking.'

The Bugle Inn, Bugle

6th June 1938, letter from Hester Parnall to A.S.B. Payne: 'I heard from Mr Barnes this morning he caught a glimpse of the sign of the Welcome Home as he passed over the Railway Bridge, and agrees with me that the white frame is hopeless, it must be black – I forgot to see if there was any old decorative iron at the Brewery which could be used to make the post look less like a gibbet…'

From an article, 'Signs of the Good Inn', in *Country Town* 1947: 'Mr Luck, general manager of the St Austell Brewery Co., says that the company's view is that inn signs should be an integral part of the countryside…"If that is so", he says, "it is worth taking trouble with the signs, designing and painting them well, and having the ironwork of the brackets made, as ours are, by a real craftsman".'

From *St Austell: Church, Town, Parish* by Dr A.L. Rowse, 1960: 'We owe a great debt to the St Austell Brewery for its visual appeal…for wherever one is in Cornwall, one can recognise its inns by the excellence of their treatment, good taste in colour-wash and paint, a really beautiful lettering in black and gold, admirably painted inn-signs by good artists under their patronage. We can recognise and be proud; for a generation now St Austell Brewery has set this good example, been a patron of the arts – to its managers we owe the pictures in the White Hart and occasional exhibitions of paintings.'

George Luck with friends at the Royal Fowey Yacht Club

The Smugglers story

One of the Brewery's most popular, and notorious, brews over the years started life as E.S.A. (Extra Strong Ale). With a barley wine flavour and an original gravity of 1060° (upped to 1070° in 1960), it was brewed for the Christmas trade in 1948 and was at first available only as a draught ale, sold at 2/4 pint. In the following year, draught sales were discontinued and it was sold instead as Smugglers Ale in 'nip' bottles at 1/- each. As Clifford Hockin commented: *'Coming as it did, after the war with its lower gravity beers, a strong ale was eagerly anticipated and received with much acclaim.'* Soon afterwards, Egbert gleefully reported to the shareholders that: *'All beer, we know, is good: can we be right in thinking that some may be a little better than others? Smugglers, "Strong Ale of Cornwall", achieved a real success, and did our resources permit, it would be tempting to see if we could not sell it beyond the Tamar against all comers. Be that as it may we had it ready in time; it was a novelty to our visitors last year for few other Breweries were then brewing a strong ale'.* In 1952 Smugglers went to London, having been chosen to stock the model village pub in the Ideal Home Exhibition at Olympia. The Smugglers story only came to an end in 1994, due to the planned closure of the bottling line. Smugglers had a fanatically loyal following, particularly down west, so how did they take the bad news? *'They've never forgiven us…'* said a Brewery insider darkly.

Smugglers Lament by D.W.E. of Fowey

From Praze-an-Beeble to Polperro, Sennen to Saltash,
There's Cornish drinkers in despair, and many teeth do gnash.
All those who liked a nifty nip,
Will surely get the blues,
When they hear the awful tidings and digest the ghastly news.

The Brewery has killed it off, and Smugglers is no more,
It's followed all the Princes who left the Cornish shore.
We liked that little bottle,
Its contents tasted right,
And half a dozen, drunk at speed, could almost make you tight!

I'll bet t'was an accountant that did the dirty deed –
Not a proper drinking man, and probably a weed!
So farewell King of Prussia,
The Lugger and the New,
For Bosun's is no substitute for what we loved and knew.

I'd like to find out who it was, and meet him on the quay.
I doubt that I'd resist the urge,
To shove him in the sea!

All was not lost, as the Smugglers name was revived in 2009 when it was used for a strong bottled ale, aged in whisky barrels, that was launched to commemorate the opening of a new bottling line at the Brewery (see page 80).

The sign of the Four Lords, St Blazey Gate

Joy Cooper painted this intriguing sign during the war. Due to various mishaps, the Brewery had had to wait for it for nearly three years. In October 1941 Joy wrote to Egbert: *'I hope your nerves are in a strong enough condition to withstand the shock of hearing that the "Four Lords" is, once more, finished and on its way to St Austell?!! My one terror is that anything should happen to it again - as easily it might, with the railways in their present condition - but it would be more than I could bear! It was extraordinarily difficult to find anywhere to paint it - once we'd left Wellington - and my hopes of doing it there were dashed, as it only arrived from the makers two days before we were going, and I had to dash to the station and square it up and draw out the design (for the guilders) on the spot… After that the guilders graciously kept it for nearly a year as, when I finally landed up here, the place was choc-a-block with evacuees! However, eventually someone died, and I managed to secure a few square feet in the middle of a lot of junk in what had once been a studio - hence the masterpiece was painted - at last! There is one important thing - it must be hung (not kept indoors) for three months and then varnished - this is vital. Also the varnish must not cover the gold, so it will have to be done very carefully…I should imagine all the others will need re-varnishing by now - they ought to be done annually without fail.'*

The design itself has excited much interest and debate over the years. The 'Four Lords' are the four main landowners in the area, whose manorial boundaries met at St Blazey Gate. As to their actual identities - well you can take your pick form the landed families of Carlyon, Edgcumbe, Rashleigh, Treffry, Pearce, Polkinghorne, Rogers and Agar-Robartes, depending on the date when the pub's name was established. The story goes that the four lords of the manors of Biscovey, Trenovissick, Roselyon and Tregrehan used to meet regularly on 'neutral ground' at this inn which was a notorious gambling den, and that on one occasion one of them lost so heavily that he had to sell a valuable ring to pay his gambling debts (hence Joy's double-sided sign which features the ring on one side but not on the other).

Steady Hands, 1939-1979

not have to do was to create or invent a visual identity for the company. They simply had to return to and reinforce something that had been in place from the early days: a concern for style and good quality that was intrinsic to the work of the Brewery's carpenters, masons, painters and signwriters.

The improvement programme was underway by 1946. In October of that year Egbert scribbled in a P.S. to a letter to Aylwin:

'Gold Leaf supplies - Have we a lot in stock? I foresee a complete re-writing of nearly all our signs.'

In the following month the Board confirmed the appointment of Mrs Betty Nagelschmidt *'to undertake responsibility for exterior decoration of the Company's properties'* and *'the adoption for all purposes of Trajan*

Column lettering', whilst noting *'that exterior decorations had been carried out at a total of approximately 60 houses in the last 18 months'.*

Joy Cooper at work

The appointment of Mrs Nagelschmidt was a bit of a *coup* for the Brewery (more specifically for Egbert Barnes, through his contacts in the art world). Better known by her maiden name of Elisabeth Benjamin, before the war she had been an architect of some distinction, a contemporary of Lubetkin and the Tecton group, much influenced by Le Corbusier and Gropius and one of the few notable female exponents of the Modern Movement in Britain. No doubt it was she who encouraged the Brewery to employ Hans Feibusch, who was well known within London architectural circles, to decorate the Ship in Fowey with exterior murals (see page 20). In an interview given in 1995 (Lynne Walker, in *Twentieth Century Architecture 2*) she recalled: *'After the war, when we were in Cornwall (1945-49), I was very friendly with Ben [Nicholson] and Barbara [Hepworth] and through them I got a job with the St Austell Brewery Company. They weren't allowed to build anything then because the restrictions were so severe, but I got out plans for development and I oversaw decoration and commissioned pub signs which was great fun.'*

The Welcome Home at Par, one of Joy Cooper's most popular signs

The Lifeboat Inn, St Ives, by signwriter Andrew Grundon

Steady Hands, 1939-1979

Several different artists were employed over the years to design and paint the pictorial pub signs that are such a distinctive feature of the Brewery's houses, including Meriel Cardew (wife of the potter Michael Cardew), Crosby Cook and, most notably and prodigiously, Joy Cooper. Particularly after the war, encouraged by Egbert and George, these modern artists were being commissioned not just to churn out a traditional Queen's Head but to use their imagination. Between them, they are responsible for some of Cornwall's most striking and familiar examples of public art.

In 1951 the Brewery celebrated its Centenary. A special Walter Hicks Centenary Ale was brewed by Mr Minchin, who had been Head Brewer since Smallwood's retirement during the war; Centenary Port and Sherry were also produced. The highlight of the celebrations for Brewery staff was a weekend trip to London to visit the Festival of Britain Exhibition, travelling in four 'char-a-bancs' and taking over an entire hotel in Kensington on the Saturday night.

Another celebratory gathering was the dinner and dance for all the Brewery's tenants and managers which was held at the Hotel Bristol in Newquay. More than 250 people attended and, among

Egbert Barnes at a wine-tasting in the cellars, 1960

the speeches, the health of the Brewery was proposed by Leslie Hawken, the landlord of the Cornish Arms at St Merryn. He presented Egbert Barnes with a clock from the managers and tenants of the company *'as a token of the high regard and esteem and deep affection in which they held the board of the company'.*

It was in this period that the wines and spirits side of the Brewery was practically reinvented. Although old Walter had been a wine and spirit merchant before he was a brewer, it had since become merely a junior element of the company with a very limited stock – mostly spirits – sold only to the Brewery houses. Although it would have been hard to foresee the extraordinary rise in popularity of wine drinking in this country in the next half century, Egbert and George had the good sense to recognise that this was an undeveloped aspect of the business that had some potential.

Tim Harvey, Walter Hick's great-grandson, was responsible for expanding and enhancing the stock out of all recognition, and for relaunching it under a rather familiar trading name. At the Board Meeting in October 1954:

'It was decided to operate the Wine and Spirit Department in future in the name of Walter Hicks & Co., primarily for the purposes of retail and private wine and spirit trade.'

'At the same time we would increase the range of wines & spirits which we bottled ourselves, and bottle a number of them under our own labels.' From the mid-'50s onwards, regular wine-tastings for free trade customers were held in the atmospheric candle-lit shadows of the cellars.

Brewery outings

The Centenary trip to London was one in a long line of annual Brewery outings, a tradition that went back to the early days. In 1925 the entire Brewery decamped to London on the train to visit the British Empire Exhibition. Clifford Hockin described how *'one of the highlights still remembered was of 'Happy' Dickie Davies ordering a pint of "Hicks" in a London pub'* (and being most put out that they hadn't heard of it...). Cecil Brewer remembered twice going to London with the Brewery in the 1930s; *'...and someone got tickets together to go to the Morris Cowley works in Oxford - they put on some do for us. Then we went up to London in the evening on the train, and went to see a show in the West End.'*

That sounds pretty civilised, but in general the outings, particularly in the '20s and early '30s, had a reputation for being riotous affairs. The usual pattern was to go by char-a-banc or train to Penzance or Plymouth, with the Brewery paying everyone's fare, plus 5/-spending money (*'quite a fair bit of money in they days'* remembers Cecil) and cigarettes or tobacco for the smokers. A letter to Hester Parnall from Mr Gillett in August 1929 hints at quite a story: *'Your staff met this morning and came to the decision to ask the Directors to allow them to fix the date of their Annual Outing for Saturday the 17th instant, this being the first day of Plymouth Naval Week. They also ask me to suggest that they be allowed to use a Char-a-banc for the journey, and would like to point out that the staff now contains no one who will be likely to abuse this privilege and cause unnecessary stops to obtain drink. It will enable them to have the chance of having a pleasant drive, as they would like to go to Plymouth via a portion of Dartmoor.'*

A county map drawn for the Brewery to mark its Centenary, 1951

Egbert's centenary speech

In his extended Chairman's Statement to the AGM in that Centenary Year, a shortened version of which he gave as his address at the Newquay dinner, Egbert dwelt at length on the achievements of his grandfather and the challenges the Brewery faced a century on: *'The Duke of Wellington, that very practical old man, still alive in 1851, used to say that "All the business of war, and indeed all the business of life, is to endeavour to find out what you don't know by what you do; that's what I call guessing what is at the other side of the hill." That is certainly our business. Compared to the very mountains in front of us how easy looks the slope which confronted Walter Hicks! No income tax, no profits tax, no death duties, no interferences by busybodies, governmental or other, no permits, no rationing; an age, in fact, of self-help with profits counted as its due reward. Further more an age of explosion, of confidence, of rising population and rising standards of living. Looking back how easy it seems! But we must remember that Walter Hicks could not see the other side of his hill, however slight a slope it now looks from here. He had few reserves and no experience; his only positive assets were enterprise, adaptability, and the courage to take risks... Conditions are different now, but the qualities we should bring to bear on them must be the same. I think I can claim them on behalf of all who are working at the brewery...They are a fine lot, a happy family and a good team. Let us be grateful to them one and all.'*

'All the business of war, and indeed all the business of life, is to endeavour to find out what you don't know by what you do; that's what I call guessing what is at the other side of the hill.'

The '125' story

In recent years the most famous product of Walter Hicks Wine Merchants has been the Walter Hicks '125' Navy Rum which, at 125° proof (71.4% vol.), is the strongest commercially-bottled rum available anywhere in the UK.

Arriving directly from Guyana in 45-gallon barrels known as hogsheads, the rum is left to mature for seven years in the Stygian gloom of the Brewery's original bonded warehouse cellars, alongside wooden cases of vintage clarets and ports. At the end of this time, some of the matured rum is broken down with water to produce the 40% vol. brand, but for the '125' it is simply bottled as it is, at full strength, with nothing added and nothing taken away. It's a wonder that the bottles don't crack…

To celebrate the Brewery's 150th anniversary the range was extended by a limited run of a 25-year-old rum at a strength of 43% vol. Only 1,212 bottles were produced from this 1975 distillation which had been maturing in hogsheads ever since, developing into a spirit of rare finesse and distinction – a must for every rum buff.

Snippets from the Board

1953/4 *'…we must unfortunately reckon on meeting the competition of TV during the coming twelve months. I am told that the craze for viewing is all absorbing for the first six months and then, as it begins to wear off, old habits and pleasure gradually reassert themselves again. If so that threat is not so serious. But the cost of the set is another matter. Hire-purchase terms involve payments of about £1 a week for 18 months, a formidable competitor for the spare cash of most working families.'*

1954/5: *'We have secured the sole agency for Cornwall of 'Coca-Cola' so that if these Cola drinks become popular we will be selling the best, and the best known, of them.'*

The Bishop & Wolf, St Mary's

Although the emphasis during this time was on consolidation and renovation rather than on buying new houses, the Brewery did make some strategic purchases in parts of the county where they had hitherto had little representation. One of these areas was the Isles of Scilly, where there was also a need for a depot to supply the free trade customers on the islands. In 1958 Egbert, George and Tim Harvey went to St Mary's to view a shop and house for sale in Hugh Town, with the idea of converting them to a public house. They reported back that *'the shop was rather on the small side but was well placed and readily convertible. There was a fair sized garden at the rear with access on to a back road, making readily feasible the provision of a wholesale store.'*

Purchase and conversion eventually cost the Brewery around £18,000, and the Bishop and Wolf opened for Whitsun 1959, bearing the name of the famous lighthouses that lie to the south-west and east, respectively, of the Scillies. The two-sided pictorial pub sign is one of Joy Cooper's most striking designs. Today regular replenishment comes by ship from Penzance Harbour.

'There was a fair sized garden at the rear with access on to a back road, making readily feasible the provision of a wholesale store.'

Steady Hands, 1939-1979

Tim remembers that *'we were trying to set up a new identity, to attract the free trade and hotels and so on, and so when we produced our first promotional material – price lists and things like that – we used elements of the family coat of arms on it.'* This was the first appearance of the 'castle', taken from the Hicks arms on the memorial tablet in Luxulyan Church, which later came to represent the Brewery as a whole and is now such a strong and recognisable symbol of the company.

Today Walter Hicks & Co. is one of the Brewery's great success stories and offers the most comprehensive selection of wines and spirits available anywhere in the West Country. As well as stocking all the big names, the company also sells its own brands: Pendennis, Tintagel and Castle D'Or sherries, Walter Hicks Gin, Montpelier Plantation White Rum, Walter Hicks Navy Rum, Sabre Vodka, Mena Dhu Whisky and Western Hunt Ruby Port. One of the reasons why Walter Hicks Wine Merchants is able, both financially and logistically, to hold such a large range of stock

is because it has its own purpose-built bonded warehouse (the only one in Cornwall) which enables huge quantities of wines to be stored with duty unpaid until the last possible minute. In 1973 the storage capacity for wines and spirits was greatly increased during major building works at the Brewery, which sadly spelt the end of the delightful garden which had been Egbert's pride and joy. A new bond was connected to the original cellars by a tunnel excavated beneath the Brewery yard. By the turn of the century, it had again been outgrown and a brand new stand-alone bonded warehouse was built behind the Brewery in June 1999. In 2009 the bonded warehouse was relocated to the new Cornwall Distribution Centre at St Columb. The current stock includes no less than 900 wines spanning all countries and all grape varieties, each one personally selected and tasted to ensure that Walter Hicks wines continue to serve every potential taste, occasion and budget.

The experimental introduction of Extra, the Brewery's first keg beer, in 1953 was *'a big innovation'*, according to Tim Harvey. *'In fact we were one of the first breweries in the country to do it. Watney's Red Barrel was the leader in that field and Watney's had a large amount of trade in Cornwall and so we thought – let's do it too! It did not really involve new technology as such – essentially it was just bottled beer in much bigger bottles – but we needed ways of dispensing it and of course new tanks for chilling and filtering (these two processes being unheard of for draught beer).'* By this time bottled beers were booming, as draught ales had an unreliable reputation; quality varied from brew to brew and they were sensitive to the differing skills of individual publicans. As Peter Voelcker, another of Walter Hicks's great-grandsons who joined the Brewery in 1959, put it:

'Unless you knew the landlord well you wouldn't risk the draught beer. Keg of course was much safer.'

Aerial view of the Brewery, late 1940s / early 1950s, showing the garden bottom left

Steady Hands, 1939-1979

Thus Extra was almost bound to be a success story, but Egbert and George were cautious at first because they were somewhat ahead of the field and the financial outlay was considerable. At a Board Meeting late in 1954, *'A report was given of the progress of the experimental stages in the production and sales of this beer. After discussion the Board decided to proceed with full-scale production, accepting the risk that the beer might be sold at the expense of our bottled beers or existing draught beers, and the outlay which would be required on plant and equipment.'* The total outlay was estimated at £20,000 – quite a steep amount for this prudent management team – but within two years it was clear that, as they had hoped, Extra was a huge hit with the free trade. As Egbert reported in 1956: *'The marketing of a stronger beer, known as Extra, and its distribution in stainless steel containers has been an unqualified success and has brought us many new accounts and customers. These containers are expensive, but they are a most convenient and hygienic way of distributing beer and of serving it in the best possible conditions.'*

Extra went down well on the national stage too. In 1960 it was on sale in London at Moore's Restaurant in Throgmorton Street and in 1976 it won a prestigious gold medal at a national beer competition run by the *Sunday Mirror*, up against 312 beers from 88 other breweries. Then in 1985 its name was changed (*'people though it sounded like a brand of petrol'*) to that old Brewery standard 'Duchy', which had been used for the bottled version of Extra since 1954.

In the early 1960s the company was shaken by the untimely deaths of two key members of staff. Ian Turnbull had been Company Secretary since 1952 and joined the Board in 1961. His sudden death at the age of 56 came only a few months after that of 42-year-old David Payne (the son of A.S.B. Payne), who had been assistant to Mr Minchin before taking over as Head Brewer in 1957. Egbert's son-in-law David Staughton was brought in on

David Staughton   Peter Voelcker   Piers Thompson

the Board, whilst Alan Izat and Clifford Hockin ably took over the roles of Head Brewer and Company Secretary, but the loss of these two men was keenly felt as Egbert made clear in this moving tribute to David Payne: *'In the first place he was a thoroughly competent Brewer and to him is due, in a very large measure, the success of Extra. The men in the Brewery respected, trusted and – it is hardly too much to say – loved him. In the Board Room we did no less, besides having a high regard for his opinion and his judgement. Off duty his charm of manner, sense of humour and sporting activities made friends wherever he went – for the Brewery as its Ambassador as well as for himself.'*

Board member Scott Seaward, left, with David Payne

Other important changes of staff at this time were the arrival in the Brewery of two more of Walter Hicks's great-grandsons: Peter Voelcker and Piers Thompson. Tim Harvey had left to pursue a career in the wine trade in London and, his workload having expanded to beyond capabilities of one man, Peter took over management of Walter Hicks & Co. whilst Piers was responsible for the Brewery's estate and free trade sales.

The Gift of the Gribbin

In 1965 the National Trust launched Enterprise Neptune, its appeal to save the coastline. In June of that year, Egbert Barnes wrote as a P.S. to his annual Chairman's Statement:

'May I commend to Shareholders' generosity the National Trust's Enterprise Neptune to save a much as possible of what is left of the Country's coastline? Nowhere is that more important than it is in Cornwall.'

Characteristically he backed up his words with action, as Michael Trinick, who ran the Trust in Cornwall, recorded in 1966: *'Mr E.C. Barnes, who is chairman of the St Austell Brewery Company which already supports our Cornwall Coast Fund with a handsome Deed of Covenant, asked if he and the company could help to buy the Gribbin, of which he is particularly fond and which can be seen in the distance from his board room.'*

The gift was completed the following year, and Egbert and the Brewery thus helped to secure one of Cornwall's loveliest headlands, one protective arm of St Austell Bay, for ever and for everyone to enjoy.

The Radjel Inn, Pendeen

On March 29th 1973 a pub called the Boscaswell Inn, which had been owned by the Brewery since 1934, was renamed The Radjel in honour of its much-loved landlord Willie Warren on his 72nd birthday. A 'radjel' means a pile of stones where a fox makes its home, and it had been the nickname of Willie's great-great-grandfather.

A large photograph of Willie Warren's beaming face hangs on the wall of the Managing Director's office in the Brewery, amongst the soberly clad directors of the past. Willie died in 1980 at the age of 79 and still holds the Brewery record for the longest-serving landlord, having run The Radjel for 59 years. It was something of a family tradition. Willie had taken on the licence after the death of his grandmother who had been the licensee since her husband died; all told, Willie's family ran the pub for 99 years. His grandfather, William Maddern, had come to the Boscaswell Inn as landlord in 1881, and Willie was brought up there after his father - who was landlord of the Star Inn, St Just - died when he was two. By the time he was fourteen Willie was working down Levant Mine, but he left to help his grandmother at the pub following the man-engine disaster of 1919 when 31 miners lost their lives.

Willie Warren behind the bar of the Radjel

Steady Hands, 1939-1979

The Brewery built its one and, so far, only purpose-built pub in 1969 just off Tregonissey Road on what was then still the eastern outskirts of St Austell. The town was beginning to grow rapidly to the east and it was recognised that a pub would be needed to serve this massive area of new housing, as well as the newly-built head office of English China Clays close by. The entire project cost £36,343 and the William Cookworthy, named in honour of the Devonian chemist who had discovered Cornwall's reserves of china clay, was opened on May 2nd. In the course of trying to decide upon a name, George Luck had written to local dignitaries asking for their opinions: one of them was that famous son of St Austell Dr A.L. Rowse, whose characteristic retort was:

'William Cookworthy? No - I think you should call it the Rowse Arms!'

In the mid-1970s the Brewery reached its peak barrelage since the war, thanks largely to exceptionally good summer weather and to the tourist boom (Cornwall's visitor numbers also peaked in the 1970s). Since that high point, the nation's traditional drink has been on the decline, nudged out by the popularity of wine and foreign lagers and the changes in social drinking brought about by the decline of heavy industry and manual labour. This was not the only fundamental change in the air as the time drew near for Egbert and George to retire. They had steered the Brewery safely through a period of major reorganisation in the brewing industry, when many small independent breweries were swallowed up by the nationals, but there was an even greater restructuring still to come. Thatcherism was on the horizon, and the mood of the country and within the business world was changing; although they had faced many challenges and difficulties in those post-war years, looking back from where we are today theirs seems by contrast to have been a gentle and a gentlemanly world.

The business principles of Egbert and George

At the AGM in 1953, Egbert gave what was in effect a statement of fundamental Brewery policy that held good for his and George Luck's entire period at the helm. In outlining how best to counter the increasing threat and competition from the national brewers, he said: *'As we see it our answer is to pursue with energy and determination the policy we have been adopting over the last few years. Our houses must be good to look at, comfortable and up to date in their amenities; our beers must be sound and well presented; we must neglect no chance of developing our valuable wine and spirit business; the sale of minerals must be expanded till it covers the county; our hotel business must not stand still for a moment. All these have been our objectives of recent years. Without them it may be safely said that our level of profits would have followed the general curve of sales in the industry. With them firmly in mind and steadily pursued we believe we can look after any competition.'*

And in 1961, these stirring words which are a fitting tribute to the era of Egbert and George: *'There are certain matters for which we owe thanks to all our staff: good management, good products, good service and, most valuable of all, the good will earned thereby. In these essential qualities we believe the small firm has advantages the huge can envy. To be best one need not to be big - as long as one remembers that the best can always be bettered. By present day standards we are a small Brewery but we are proud of the beers we brew and of the wines we sell, of our Houses, of the men and women who work for us and of the reputation we believe these things have brought us. We hope that you are too.'*

The Brewery staff float in St Austell Carnival, 1949

The Brewery, 1979

Pedn-Olva Hotel, St Ives, bought in 1999

Chapter V
Growing & Brewing, 1979-2001

In 1979 Egbert was succeeded as Chairman by his son-in-law David Staughton, and Piers Thompson took over from George Luck as Managing Director. George's son Adam Luck, meanwhile, had joined the Brewery in 1975 with responsibility for the tenanted trade, and in 1980 James Staughton (Walter Hicks's great-great grandson) came in on the wines and spirits side.

In this new age, which was altogether more demanding and competitive, it was time for the Brewery's priorities to shift and develop. Egbert and George had created a solid foundation; the estate of pubs and hotels was in good order and the company finances were sound, thanks to their intrinsic prudence. Now Piers and his fellow directors (initially just his cousin Peter Voelcker, but joined by Michael Ruthven in 1987 who came with wide brewing and retail experience) could see that the business needed to grow in order to survive and go forward.

The first area of growth was in the Brewery's estate, which had expanded very little since the war. This meant not simply buying more pubs, but having a strategic policy. Piers had already made some key acquisitions such as the Pandora Inn at Restronguet, the Great Western Hotel at Newquay and the Old Customs House at

The Victoria Inn, Salcombe, bought in 2001

The Punchbowl and Ladle, Feock, bought in 2001

Padstow which were proving to be very successful; now the Brewery looked to expand into Devon. In the next twenty years depots serving the free trade were opened up in Ilfracombe, through buying the Drink Link company, and in Newton Abbot, and fifteen Devonian houses were bought – the furthest east being the Mill on the Exe at Exeter. At the start of 2001 the Brewery bought its 152nd pub – the Victoria Inn in Salcombe – for £1 million; whatever would Walter Hicks have made of that? Hand in hand with acquisition went a programme of investment in the larger managed houses to allow them to reach their full potential and to keep pace with the increased expectations of their customers. Pubs like the Central in Newquay, the Old Customs House in Padstow and, more recently, the Pedn-Olva Hotel in St Ives have had considerable sums spent on their redevelopment, with immediate returns justifying the expenditure.

Growing & Brewing, 1979-2001

Growth in business was the next priority to be addressed and in 1993 the Brewery took one of the most significant steps in its history when it bought Carlsberg-Tetley's wholesale business in Cornwall and the Isles of Scilly. In an era increasingly dominated by choice and diversity, this major investment has allowed the Brewery to compete profitably in the free trade as composite wholesalers, with the ability to supply its customers with all their liquid requirements in one delivery. *'It was the biggest single change in our direction'* recalls Adam Luck of the Carlsberg-Tetley deal, for which the Brewery could thank Piers Thompson's *'vision, sound business sense and extraordinarily good judgement'*. James Staughton was responsible for mastering the complex deal itself. *'It meant that we could go to free houses and clubs, not only with our brands to offer them, but the national brands which are Carlsberg-Tetley products, and then say: this is what we've got to offer. It's given us a wide portfolio, and it has been incredibly successful.'*

As the new millennium approached, and more and more independent breweries ceased brewing in the face of competition from national and international brands, the Brewery had to reassess where it was and how it fitted in to the modern industry.

Gone for ever was the era of thousands of small breweries scattered across the country, each with their own estate of pubs and a dependable local beer market. Enormous volumes were brewed back then because beer was practically a staple diet and the customer was not exactly faced with a vast array of alternatives when he walked into his local: you were either a mild man or a bitter man and that's the way you stayed. By 2001 St Austell was one of around 35 independent regional family breweries still brewing (today the number is 28), and in addition it faced a particular challenge common to all Cornish businesses reliant on wild fluctuations in seasonal demand. Yet to brew or not to brew was never really the question, for it has always been understood by everyone – the Board, the staff, the shareholders – that brewing is the very heart and soul of this company. Instead, the Brewery recommitted itself to the art of brewing premium ales, with the focus on quality right the way through from raw materials to output and service.

In 1999 a new Head Brewer, Roger Ryman, was appointed by James Staughton and he brought with him a belief in the inherent strengths of regional breweries and a confidence in the power and value of a good product. *'Making beer is like making anything else. Take a steak for instance: if you've got a good piece of meat you can easily ruin it, but you'll never get a great steak out of a bad piece of meat. You have to start off with the best possible materials for brewing.'* The key materials to get right, along with the water and yeast,

Laboratory technician – monitoring the brewing process

Roger Ryman

Continued on page 61

The pull of a good pint

Letter to the *Cornish Guardian* from Cyril Thompson of Fowey, August 1981: *'A disaster has struck the people of Cornwall. Our adorable St Austell Brewery has increased the price of its excellent beer by 3p per pint. Thousands, including myself, will have no option than to join a club or form social clubs where we can get our couple of pints 4p to 5p cheaper. We all know the quality of the beer that this family brewery have brewed for years, but they must understand that people cannot afford to pay the price tag on their products. So farewell to all St Austell brewery houses, until the day you decide to reduce your beer to a reasonable price. We shall all be wearing black ties, and going into mourning for one month, out of respect for the excellent service, beautiful beer and comfort of the St Austell Brewery pubs, which we have all enjoyed for so many years and which we are now deprived of by the abominable, diabolical, outrageous 3p per pint increase. One man's loss is another man's gain in the brewery trade.'*

Letter to the *Cornish Guardian* from Mr Cyril Thompson of Fowey, September 1981: *'Recently I wrote a letter complaining about the 3p increase in the price of a pint of St Austell Brewery's beer. I stated that I would never again drink this beer. But I am a man of honour and never afraid to stand corrected. I feel I have made a mistake. The price of beer in the club bars may be a few pence cheaper. But after visiting a number of clubs I have gone back to my beloved pint of wonderful and delicious St Austell brew...and back to my local public house. I was only away for a week – but how I missed my excellent landlord and landlady. Now I am happily and contentedly back in the fold.'*

The copper (1914-1998)

Farewell to old friends?

In 1998 the old 100-barrel copper, which had been boiling away steadily since 1914, was replaced by a stainless steel giant with a 150-barrel capacity. Unlike the two original steam-heated 40-barrel coppers (no longer in use) this one had been coal-fired, presumably because at the time of the 1912-1914 expansion the Brewery's boilers were not large enough to cope with the increased workload. In this great open cauldron, built into a kiln made from 10,000 local bricks (it received a copper lid in 1947 and was later converted to steam), the wort and hops were boiled over a constantly-tended coal fire for an hour and a half. In between brews the copper was scrubbed out by hand using two buckets of fine sand; for this gruelling work the boilermen were given double the daily allowance of pale ale (two quarts). At the end of its working life, the copper lived on through recycling: it was used to make commemorative copper coins to celebrate the Brewery's 150th anniversary.

As various elements of the Brewery have been replaced or renewed over the years, so some have inspired more nostalgia than others. Few people in St Austell went into mourning when the old boiler chimney began to be dismantled, brick by brick, in November 1980. It was a thing of beauty - tall, elegant, tapering to slenderness, a typical Victorian decorative brick stack which had graced the skyline for nearly 90 years - but it had fallen from favour with local people since it started depositing clouds of sooty smuts onto their cars, houses, children, dogs and clean washing. Unable to cure the problem, the Brewery had to replace it with a 100ft steel stack, in a different position, bypassing the underground flues. It worked - it was efficient, clean, economical, and sensible - but no one could ever have accused it of being beautiful. In 2001, with the advent of more fuel-efficient technology, it was in its turn replaced by a 35ft stack and a single boiler system.

Slightly more nostalgia accompanied the passing of the Brewery steam hooter in 2000. No longer needed in an age when the constraints of old working practices had loosened, it was nonetheless a familiar and dependable feature of local life from Polgooth to Charlestown to Tregrehan (depending on the wind direction); a part of the aural landscape. It wasn't just the Brewery staff who stopped for crib when the 10 o' clock hooter went. Who knows how many lives revolved unconsciously around its regular wheezy blasts, and how many internal clocks were disorientated when it finally fell silent? *'We have relied on this wonderful sound so much.'* wrote a St Austell resident to the *Western Morning News*:

'...especially the 7am hoot, but without the lunchtime and 4pm friendly sounds we feel quite lost.'

The brewing process

Sometimes referred to as the world's second oldest profession, brewing in one form or other has long been an everyday part of life in the British Isles. The Roman writer Pliny wrote of the fondness of western Europeans for a drink made from corn and water:

Malted barley, at the top of the tower

'So exquisite is the cunning of mankind in gratifying their vicious appetites that they have thus invented a method to make water itself intoxicating.'

Walter Hicks's splendid old mill of 1890 worked continuously until 2011, when it went into retirement

Another Roman wrote that Celts in Britain steeped and germinated grain,by which its spirits were excited and set free; it was then dried, ground, and infused in water when, after fermentation, it produced a pleasant, warming, strengthening and intoxicating liquor. Until the emergence of purpose-built brewhouses in the eighteenth century, brewing was largely a domestic activity carried out in farm and cottage kitchens, in monasteries, great houses, colleges and, later, taverns. Beer was the everyday drink for all ages. Brewing was as normal an activity

as baking bread and, like bread-making, the fundamental process remains much the same as it ever was even if the tools of the trade have changed with the times. The traditional tower system of brewing, still in use at St Austell, starts with the initial ingredients being pumped or hoisted to the highest point of the brewery, and from here progress from one stage to the next is governed by the force of gravity.

MILLING: In the mill at the very top of the tower, malted barley is ground to break down the outer walls of the grains to produce 'grist': a coarse flour.

Temperature being checked in the mash tun

MASHING: In the mash tun on the floor below the mill, the grist is mixed with 'liquor', as water is called throughout the brewing process, which has been heated to 74°C. The grist and liquor enter the mash tuns together at a temperature of around 65°C, heaving and plopping occasionally like porridge on a stove and smelling of hot sweet biscuits. The 'goods', as the grist and liquor mixture is known, now stand in the tuns for an hour, during which time a fermentable malty sugary solution is extracted from the grains.

SPARGING: After the stand, the goods are 'sparged' (sprayed with hot liquor which permeates down through the goods and extracts the malty sugars from them). The solution produced by sparging is known as 'sweet wort'; it is the colour of honey and tastes like malt syrup. Sparging continues until the required amount of wort has been drawn off from the bottom of the tun, from where it is pumped to the 'copper'. The spent grist is sold as cattle feed.

BOILING: The copper, a massive steam-heated cauldron, is where the hops are added to the wort and boiled for 1¼ hours to extract bitterness from the hops, to sterilise the wort, and to remove any unwanted proteins. A portion of the hops is kept back and added at the end of the boil, to enhance the hoppy aroma of the beers. From the copper the wort is pumped to the 'whirlpool'. As it swirls around the whirlpool vessel, wort solids and hops are drawn to the bottom allowing crystal clear wort to be decanted from above. At this stage, for some beers, this clear wort is sparged over a bed of finest aromatic hops in a vessel called the 'hop back', to extract the fine hoppy flavour. Spent hops are mixed with the spent grist for cattle feed.

COOLING: This is a critical part of the process as the temperature of the wort needs to be driven down from around 90°C to 18°C before the yeast can be added. Once cooled, the wort is pumped to the fermenting vessels.

FERMENTING: Yeast is the magic ingredient of beer. This mysterious living fungus transforms the wort in spectacular fashion, the foaming head of the yeast on top of the wort being a striking indication of the frantic activity taking place beneath. The yeast's main job is to convert the sugar in the wort to alcohol and carbon dioxide. By tradition, the beer stays in the fermenting vessels for a week because *'any beer that had not been blessed by the Sabbath is deemed ungodly'*.

Cask racking

Bottles ready to be filled

THE FINISHED PRODUCTS:

Traditional cask-conditioned beers - HSD, Proper Job, Tribute, Trelawny, Dartmoor Best, Black Prince plus the seasonal beers - are simply 'racked' (filled into casks). This living beer undergoes a secondary fermentation in the cask, bringing the beer into 'condition'. At this stage, 'finings' (a collagen extracted from the swim bladders of certain tropical fish!) are added to help the beer settle when it is 'stillaged' at the pub. Today, casks are made of stainless steel, although the Brewery does still supply one pub, the St Kew Inn, with beer in traditional wooden casks.

Bottled beers - see page 70 for the full list - are conditioned in tanks for 7 to 14 days after fermentation, before being filtered to yield crystal clear 'bright beer' which is gently carbonated prior to filling. St Austell doesn't pasteurise its bottled beers, which helps to retain the clean brewery-fresh taste, and a number of its beers are dosed with live yeast, like champagne, and undergo a secondary fermentation in the bottle to achieve the natural condition, or gentle sparkle in the finished beer. Amber bottles are selected to protect the beer from sunlight, which can damage the flavour.

Fermenting vessels - adding St Austell Brewery's unique yeast

The cask ale range in 2011

Tribute

'A month after its launch it was the Brewery's best selling beer'

Tribute started life as Daylight Robbery, a short-term seasonal beer brewed to celebrate the total eclipse of the sun in August 1999. Its phenomenal success came as something of a surprise, not least to Roger Ryman: *'It was the first new beer I'd brewed at St Austell. I was used to producing new beers every two months at Maclays [the Scottish brewery where Roger had been Assistant Head Brewer]; they were made, they sold and we moved on. With Daylight I just thought that's a nice pint, that's good and then it just went ballistic. It had a great name and the timing was good, but a month after its launch it was the Brewery's best selling beer and sales carried on like that for the rest of the summer and into the autumn'.* Daylight had made itself indispensable; by virtue of its success and popularity it promoted itself from the ephemeral to the permanent and in 2001 was relaunched as one of the Brewery's core brands under its new name: **Tribute**. See page 68 for what happened next!

The unforgettable smell of a brewery at work

Lynn Pearson identified in *British Breweries: an Architectural History* what she calls *'the emotional impact of that distinctive hoppy aroma'*, and no-one describes this better than Dr A. L. Rowse who attended St Austell Grammar School in the early 1900s: *'...and then there was that more exotic scent from the Brewery next door, of malt or hops or of I do not know what aromatic spices they used in brewing, which the west wind blew across our playing fields, enveloping the school in its warm, soft, sweet, drowsy, liquorous smell, that insinuated itself into the passages and corridors and classrooms, came in puffs at the windows, lurked heavily about the lower quarters of the school - and, in short, so wound itself into my mind that often when I think of those school days the memory of that nostalgic smell is entwined with them'.* (From *A Cornish Childhood*)

'The emotional impact of that distinctive hoppy aroma'

Clouded Yellow has landed

Like Daylight Robbery, the success of Clouded Yellow took everyone by surprise; indeed you could almost say it caught them on the hop. This distinctive beer, in the style of a German wheat beer, was one of several experimental one-off brews created by Roger for the first Celtic Beer Festival in 1999. Just two barrels were made and it went down well at the festival under the unofficial name of Hagar the Horrible. *'Then the Tesco Beer Challenge came up'*, as Roger recalled:

'...and they were looking for innovative beers so I bunged some in a bottle and sent it off just for fun.'

It was with a mixture of alarm and delight that he discovered it had won first prize and the Brewery had just five weeks to develop it commercially and get it ready for Tesco to distribute nationwide through its supermarkets. Moreover, no-one else in the Brewery management knew he had entered it in the competition, and it didn't even have a name. Eventually they picked Clouded Yellow from a book of British butterflies because it suited the look and style of the beer and they wanted a bright, summery image on the label. In addition, they liked the apt description of the butterfly as *'a migrant: it is most common in the South but reaches all parts of the British Isles'.* As St Austell's first nationally-distributed beer it has gone down very well; it has won many plaudits including coming top in a *Which?* magazine tasting of bottle-fermented beers *('a golden, refreshing beer, our panelists praised it for its typical wheat beer flavours such as spice, apples and particularly bananas').*

Growing & Brewing, 1979-2001

Continued from page 58

are malt and hops. The Brewery uses premium quality Maris Otter malt, some of which still comes from Tuckers Maltings in Newton Abbot in keeping with company policy to use local suppliers where possible. Tuckers is a small business that celebrated its centenary in 2000; of all its original brewery customers back in 1900, St Austell Brewery is the only one which still exists. It is also vitally important to use the finest hops, and different varieties are used to impart different flavours to the beers. For HSD and Black Prince, Fuggles and Goldings are used – traditional old-fashioned English hops grown in Herefordshire – but with some of the newer beers Roger is experimenting with varieties from overseas, including New Zealand and America:

'For Tribute, Proper Job and IPA we use hops from Washington and Oregon – they have a very citrusy, tangy flavour which comes across in those beers, whereas English hops tend to be drier.'

What is the popular image of a traditional Head Brewer? Someone in his fifties maybe, portly and grey-haired in a tweed jacket, a blunt no-nonsense character who likes a few drinks, a bit domineering in the brewhouse perhaps, someone to be feared as well as respected. In the realm of mash tuns and fermenting vessels, he is king. There is an ancient mystique surrounding the brewing of beer; it even has its own language peppered with Anglo-Saxon words – wort, grist, liquor, the goods, finings, racking, sparging – which is impenetrable to outsiders. Roger Ryman does not exactly fit the picture of the typical Head Brewer of the past, and as for his profession's tendency to shroud itself in mystery, he says *'brewers are second only to car mechanics for making something simple seem complicated'*.

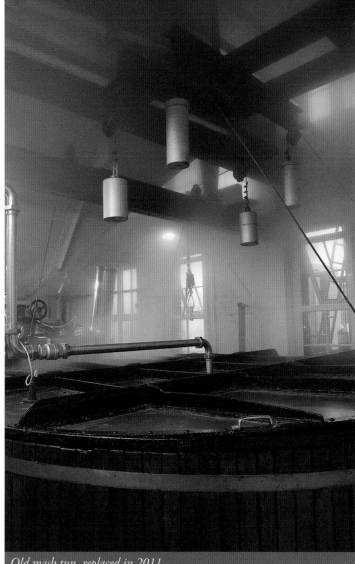

Old mash tun, replaced in 2011

Yet there is no escaping the feeling, when you catch that sweet and heady smell on the wind on brewing days, that something magical like alchemy must be going on inside those brewhouse walls. Part of this mystique comes from the fact that brewing is both an art and a science. As Roger says, it is *'a life science. All the basic processes of life are there in brewing. A lot of early research by Louis Pasteur and others, breaking down the actual biochemistry of life, was done in breweries. But it is also an art in that there's always a place for flair, and the good thing about working in a brewery like St Austell is that you've got the scope to use it.'*

Growing & Brewing, 1979-2001

Following Roger's arrival, the Brewery made a commitment both to its four core draught ales (at that time: HSD, Tinners, Tribute and IPA) and to a seasonal beer programme based on six new short-term brews a year, which are particularly popular with the free trade. In addition, the Brewery was then still producing XXXX Mild which won a CAMRA Best Beer award in 1990 and was one of the few remaining draught milds still being brewed in the country. In keg, Duchy was still going strong, alongside Cornish Cream and Celtic Smooth. At the end of this period, in 2001, only two bottled beers were being produced – HSD and the award-winning Clouded Yellow. The bottling took place at the Brakspear (Oxfordshire) and Redruth breweries, since the closure of St Austell's bottling line in 1995.

In 1992 the Brewery opened its first Visitor Centre, catering to a growing interest not just in beer and brewing generally, but a specific interest amongst tourists and locals alike in the history of this old family firm. In its early days, the Visitor Centre included an off-licence, sample bar and gift shop, as well as offering guided tours of the Brewery.

In December 1999 the Brewery hosted its first Celtic Beer Festival, featuring draught ales and lagers from Cornwall, Scotland, Ireland, Wales, the Isle of Man and Brittany, and music from Cornish bands and choirs. Held in the atmospheric surroundings of the Brewery cellars and the old bonded warehouse, linked together by the tunnel, the festival was a hugely successful celebration of Celtic pride and excellent brewing. It has since become an annual event.

In April 2000 James Staughton became Managing Director of the Brewery on Piers Thompson's retirement. Piers in turn succeeded James's father David Staughton, as Chairman. As Walter Hicks's great-great grandson, James is the fifth generation of the Hicks family to be actively involved in running St Austell Brewery, along with his cousin Piers Thompson junior who joined in 1993. Another cousin William Michelmore was appointed to the Board in 1996 as a non-executive director. This is a remarkable dynastic achievement for any business, and it is at the heart of the Brewery's success as one of the great Cornish companies. Its essential stability comes from this continuity not just of family ownership but of family management. As well as having more remote relationship as shareholders, Walter's descendents have always worked in the Brewery and for the Brewery, and therein lies the strength. Like those Victorian gardeners who planted trees for another generation to enjoy, the Managing Director sees himself as a custodian; rather than sweating whatever he can out of the company for short-term gain, he takes the long view, with a perspective shaped by both the past and the future.

Annual Celtic Beer Festival, raising over £10,000 each year for St Austell Brewery's Charitable Trust

'Its essential stability comes from this continuity not just of family ownership but of family management.'

The HSD story

Probably St Austell Brewery's most famous brand over the years, and certainly its most infamous, Hicks Special Draught started life in 1975.

The possibility of producing a *'good strength and comparatively expensive Draught Bitter from the Wood'* was first discussed by George Luck, Piers Thompson and the Head Brewer Alan Izat two years earlier. In the summer of '75 the Board agreed that Alan's *experimental brews of a high quality naturally conditioned draught beer at 1050° should be tried out in 20 – 30 tied houses on a pilot basis. It would be called Hicks's Special Draught and it was envisaged that it would sell at 26p a pint'.*

Despite its subsequent success, HSD was a tricky brew at first and had a rather rocky start. Adam Luck, who had just started at the Brewery, remembers it vividly: *'It was troublesome, problematical, difficult for landlords to handle…. So we withdrew it to get it right and then relaunched it the following year and it's been a huge success ever since. It's now considered to be a key brand because it is so unusual – it is markedly different to other beers.'* Hicks Special Draught was produced in half-pint bottles as Jubilee Ale in 1977, to celebrate the Queen's Silver Jubilee, and today is bottled as HSD.

HSD's distinctive taste and *'a certain reputation as one that's going to knock you over',* as Roger Ryman puts it, have given it something of a cult following over the years and spawned a number of nicknames including Hicks's Sudden Death and High Speed Diesel.

'A certain reputation as one that's going to knock you over'

The dying art of the cooper

Bill Hockin

Pictured left is Bill Hockin, father of Clifford Hockin who has been mentioned and quoted many times in this story. Bill was Head Cooper at the Brewery from the early years of the twentieth century.

The Brewery's last cooper was Llew Jones, who ran the cooper's shop from 1977 until his retirement in 2001. Interviewed by the *Western Morning News* in 1995 to celebrate his 40 years in the coopering trade, Llew explained how it took him about a day to make a nine gallon firkin: *'We mainly use old hogshead rum barrels from Guyana which we cut up to make smaller casks. That way we don't waste good wood,* and the steaming and hot fires – which are part of the making process – help to disperse the rum flavouring of the wood. The skills of the cooper still lie in the use of some 22 tools. All the work is done by eye, I don't measure anything.'

Llew Jones

CHAPTER VI
A NEW MILLENNIUM BEGINS
2001-2011

'As the rockets explode during the firework display, cheer not only in celebration of our achievements but also cheer for our families and friends before us, in recognition of their past achievements for the Company.'

Extract from James Staughton's welcome speech at the 150th anniversary celebrations

The five previous chapters charted the story of
St Austell Brewery's history from its beginnings in
the enterprise and drive of one man – Walter Hicks
– to its 150th anniversary in 2001. They formed
the core of the original book *Brewing for Cornwall*,
which was written to celebrate that anniversary.

As that book drew to a close, the Brewery was looking forward to
celebrating the momentous milestone of its 150th anniversary, and the
celebrations were done in some style. There was a huge staff party held
in a marquee at John Keay House (now part of Cornwall College), with
fireworks, feasting and dancing. The highlight of the 150th anniversary
was the long-awaited visit to the Brewery of His Royal Highness Prince
Charles, the Duke of Cornwall (see next page for a personal recollection
of the day, and page 90 for his original Foreword to *Brewing for Cornwall*).

Now, ten years on, it's hard to believe that so much has happened to
the world around us, as well as to the Brewery. The pace of change itself
is so much faster than it was even a decade ago, with so many exciting
developments in the Brewery, that it is time – as the company approaches
its 160th anniversary – for the book to be re-launched and another chapter
to be written to bring the story up to date, and to look forward to the
future of one of Cornwall's most famous and successful businesses.

This family company, founded firmly in the spirit and principles of the
distant, unfamiliar world of Victorian England, looks remarkably well-
placed to take on all the challenges of a very different age, as we broach
the second decade of the 21st century.

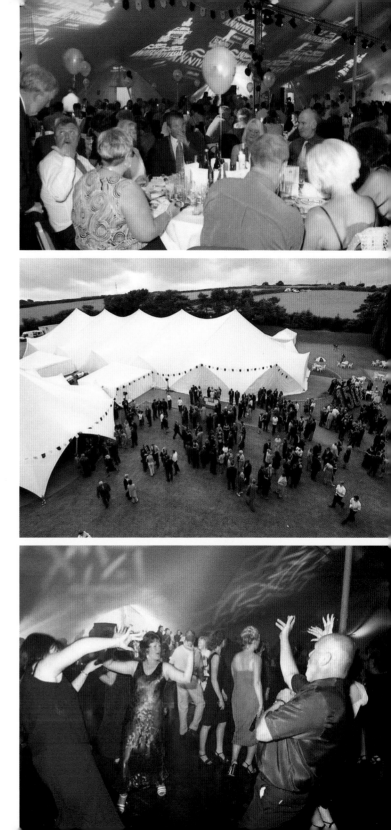

MEMORIES OF PRINCE CHARLES'S VISIT

By Vicky Crossingham, Estate Recruitment Director until 2011

'Local dignitaries, employees and their families, brewery pensioners and primary schoolchildren formed a welcoming party in the brewery yard (the Prince later made time to speak to several of them, after unveiling the plaque, and won many hearts that day). On his arrival he was greeted by James and taken on a brewery tour. He appeared fascinated by the whole brewing process and spoke to workers on his way around. Like most visitors at that time, the Prince found our cooper Llew Jones's demonstration highly entertaining and laughed uproariously at Llew's demonstration of his 'knocking up' stick.

'At last the Prince arrived at the Visitor Centre, where the Senior Team was introduced to him. I was amazed at his knowledge and he talked at length to me about the set up of the Visitor Centre. (Imagine my surprise in meeting him months later at St Dennis, when he recognised me from his visit to the brewery!). The Prince then signed a copy of our brewery history book, for which he'd written the Foreword, and was delighted to meet the author Liz Luck (I remember clearly those in the Visitor Centre remarking on Liz's beautiful legs as she was wearing a very pretty shortish frock), along with Laurence Sutherland who designed the book and John Preston who helped with the research.

'Prince Charles agreed to a photoshoot of him behind the bar pulling a pint. Just imagine Roger's chagrin when the Prince pulled a glass full of froth and exclaimed: 'It's all foam and no beer!' Our fault – we'd been so busy testing the quality of the beer in the cellar that we forgot to pour off the first pint in readiness. When Diana Luck said to me: "He will make a wonderful king", I replied: "A fine king but a lousy barman!"'

'A fine king but a lousy barman!'

A NEW MILLENNIUM BEGINS, 2001-2011

A brewing revolution

Ten years ago the Brewery had not long appointed a new Head Brewer (see page 56 onwards), who had already scored a notable success with his creation of Tribute. Since those auspicious beginnings, it is no exaggeration to say that Roger Ryman and his brewing team have transformed the Brewery's fortunes. Roger is now widely acknowledged to be one of this country's leading brewers, and was voted Brewer of the Year in 2008 by the All-Party Parliamentary Beer Group. What is known as the 'Roger Ryman effect' has brought about one of the biggest revolutions and success stories in the company's history.

Roger Ryman and the brewing team

Put simply: ten years ago, beer was being brewed three times a week; for much of 2010 (and for the first time in the history of the Brewery), beer was brewed three times a *day*. The nearly 60,000 brewers' barrels brewed in 2010 beat the previous record set in the 1970s (when beer was still seen as Britain's traditional drink with little competition, and Cornwall was at its peak of popularity as a tourist destination). The scale of this success is even more staggering when viewed in the context of the world of today – a very different landscape to the 1970s.

In a decade, the Brewery's annual sales of its own cask ales have tripled, and now stand at over 16.7 million pints a year.

New mash tun installed March 2011

Here is the key: Roger and his team have created and brewed consistently popular and award-winning beers – 23 beer awards were won in 2010 alone. The Tribute story has been an extraordinary tale of stratospheric growth and success, but it is not the only beer setting the pace…

Proper Job is now the Brewery's second-bestselling cask ale, a traditional highly hopped golden citrusy IPA that Roger created in 2006.

HSD is St Austell's most legendary ale and remains hugely popular: full-bodied and strong, brimming with a kaleidoscope of flavours. Brewed with plenty of malt and lashings of English Fuggles and Golding hops, HSD is truly a classic ale of considerable depth and complexity.

What next? A brand new beer joined the party to mark the Brewery's 160th anniversary in June 2011. Named Trelawny, this full-flavoured yet easy drinking 3.8% cask ale is copper-coloured with a notable malt character, overlaid with a classic hop flavour from English Golding hops, and a refreshing zest that comes from the distinctive Galaxy hops imported from Launceston, Tasmania.

Investment in the Brewery's plant has gone hand-in-hand with the resurgence of brewing. In the 2001 book we were talking about the replacement of the old 1914 copper (see page 57); ten years on, with new mash tuns and grain silo installed in March 2011, every piece of brewing equipment at every stage of the brewing process is now less than a decade old.

'*Tribute is a magnificent example of a bronze coloured English bitter, with a rich aroma of biscuity malt and tart citrus fruit from the Willamette hops.*'

TRIBUTE TAKES OFF

It's hard to believe that it was only ten years ago that we wrote: '…in 2001 Daylight Robbery was relaunched as one of the Brewery's core brands under its new name "Tribute"' (see page 60). In the intervening decade, Tribute has become St Austell Brewery's first truly national beer, its flagship product and the driving force behind this venerable old Cornish company's reinvigorated success.

A national sales team was formed in 2001 to take Tribute to pub companies, wholesalers and supermarkets throughout the UK. Not only has it been voted the South West's favourite beer, it is ranked in the top 20 of the UK's premium cask ales. Tribute accounts for an astonishing 70% of the Brewery's beer sales, and is the top product in the company's entire portfolio – outstripping the volume sales even of Carlsberg lager. Notable fans of Tribute include Roger Protz, editor of the *Good Beer Guide*, who wrote '*Tribute is a magnificent example of a bronze coloured English bitter, with a rich aroma of biscuity malt and tart citrus fruit from the Willamette hops. Juicy malt, hop resins and tangy fruit coat the tongue, while the finish is long and lingering, with a fine balance between malt, hops and fruit, finally becoming dry and bitter.*'

Tribute is also the proud sponsor of the Rugby Football Union leagues in Devon, Cornwall and Somerset as well as official beer of the Cornish Pilot Gig Association.

A NEW MILLENNIUM BEGINS, 2001-2011

Bottling returns to the Brewery

Since the 150th anniversary book was written all the bottling of our beers has taken place at other breweries, some of them far away from Cornwall. Sixteen years since the old bottling line was closed there is now a new state-of-the-art bottling line at the Brewery: how Walter Hicks would have loved that! It was opened in July 2009 by the Lord Lieutenant of Cornwall Lady Mary Holborow, with all the Brewery pensioners invited to the celebrations. New labels were designed to mark the occasion, and all bottles now have international labelling, opening the door for the Brewery to export its bottled ales.

Lady Mary Holborow opening the new bottling line in 2009

This significant return to bottling has been encouraged by the shift in the UK's drinking habits, with more people choosing to drink in their homes rather than in licensed houses, by the growing interest in matching beer with food, and by the ever increasing popularity and availability of St Austell ales in supermarkets. From an environmental perspective, too, it clearly makes good green sense not to have to transport beers in road tankers to bottling plants up country.

Having a bottling line on site encourages innovation, and in 2010 the Brewery launched Korev Cornish Lager, a high-quality bottom-fermented lager, brewed to authentic central European standards. Alongside Korev, the other beers now bottled at St Austell are Tribute, Proper Job, HSD, Admiral's Ale, Clouded Yellow and Smugglers, with additional one-off brews enabling innovation to take place to ensure St Austell Brewery can be well placed for the future and ahead of market trends.

Brewery pensioners celebrating the opening of the bottling line

Cornwall's long been known for great pasties, saffron cakes and clotted cream (and beer, of course) but hand-in-hand with its recent resurgence as a desirable holiday destination has come its rebirth as one of the UK's gastronomic high-spots.

Visitors now know that if they come to Cornwall, they're going to be able to find both really good local food to buy, and exceptional meals to enjoy at restaurants, cafés and pubs.

Some of the country's most famous chefs have set up shop here, and the ripple effect of their high standards, insistence on the best local ingredients and attention to detail has spread throughout the county. Godfather to them all, of course, is Rick Stein who opened his first restaurant in Padstow back in 1974. In 2009 he took on the lease of his first St Austell Brewery pub – the Cornish Arms at St Merryn – which he runs not as a gastro-pub but as a proper local with really good unfussy pub food using the best local ingredients (see his message of congratulation on page 87).

In 2008 St Austell Brewery was awarded national Food Pub Company of the Year at the Publican Food and Drink Awards, in recognition of its success in developing and delivering outstanding food throughout the Brewery's pubs, using local foods from local suppliers and growers.

Many St Austell Brewery pubs have taken local sourcing to their hearts, and won awards for the quality of their food.

Cornwall is well placed to make the most of a growing popular interest in - and demand for - fresh, high quality local and seasonal foods, with the sea on its doorstep and an abundance of excellent dairy and market garden produce. Many St Austell Brewery pubs have taken local sourcing to their hearts, and won awards for the quality of their food. The Brewery is a member of Cornwall Catering Excellence and sponsors the annual Cornwall Food and Drink Festival on Lemon Quay in Truro.

A NEW MILLENNIUM BEGINS, 2001-2011

Cool Cornwall

Think back to 2001, and it's amazing to consider how much the image of Cornwall has changed in a decade. The economic waters might be choppy and cold right now, but Cornwall remains a hot destination – and not just for one type of visitor; increasingly it's seen as having something to offer everyone – from cool camping to the most stylish award-winning hotels. You can't open a Sunday supplement without seeing one celebrity or another naming Cornwall as their favourite place. There seems to be a magic in the name – it's like a talisman. Of course, it's been a popular holiday destination since the mid-nineteenth century (see page 17), but something has changed recently. Cornwall's fame has shifted up a few gears – perhaps the quality of food, drink and accommodation has taken a leap forward, whilst its natural wild beauty and its distinctive history and character remain a huge draw – but for whatever reason, there is no doubt that Cornwall is currently deeply cool.

The spectacularly successful Eden project was launched in 2000, and since then has welcomed more than 11 million visitors; the National Maritime Museum Cornwall opened in Falmouth in 2003, and the Tate St Ives is currently undergoing a major expansion. Newquay airport has been expanded too, with flights from many cities throughout the country making Cornwall easy to reach for weekends and short breaks.

Newquay itself has become the country's number one hotspot for weekend party goers, with bars and clubs to rival the best that the Mediterranean has to offer.

The Central Inn is the Brewery's busiest pub, and with refurbishments in 2005 and 2010 it has positioned itself at the leading edge of the UK's style bars. Other Cornish towns like Padstow and St Ives might attract a different crowd, but they too have become year-round weekend break destinations, with Friday nights as vibrant and busy in November as they are in July.

The relentless rise in the popularity of surfing and extreme sports has sealed the ultra-trendy reputation of Cornwall and North Devon, whilst technological improvements in wetsuits, and their general availability, have opened up the sea to hardy visitors throughout the year.

Meanwhile, Cornwall's traditional industries, particularly fishing and mining, have continued to struggle. St Austell as a town has owed much of its development to the china clay industry (see page 9), but this has been a tough decade that saw much of the clay extraction moved from Cornwall to Brazil, and many local people working in the china clay business have lost their jobs. St Austell and its surrounding villages have been hit hard, and it's only recently, as new investment in the town begins to bear fruit with a new cinema and town centre being built and new shops and restaurants opening, that things have started to look brighter. Indeed St Austell now finds itself at the forefront of Cornwall's development, having been chosen as the location for two eco-towns which will rejuvenate sites formerly used to serve the clay mining industry. In addition, the long-awaited and controversial development of the Carlyon Bay beach area will further boost the town's economy.

There is no doubt that Cornwall is currently deeply cool

The Central Inn, Newquay

Old Customs House, Padstow

Andreya Wharry, kitesurfing record holder, 2004

Old Market House, Brixham

Hope and Anchor, Hope Cove

A NEW MILLENNIUM BEGINS, 2001-2011

Down at your local

Never mind the changes to Cornwall in the last decade, what about the revolution that has taken place in the world of the pub?

Perhaps nothing in the history of the public house has had a more profound impact than the national smoking ban, which came into effect in 2006. Smokers now congregate in beer gardens or specially erected shelters, and whilst many customers have enjoyed bidding farewell to the old smoky public bar, there have been a few unexpected revelations such as the lingering odours from cooking or cleaning products that were previously masked. The role of an open fire in creating atmosphere and a welcoming smell of burning wood or coal has never been more critical!

The combined effect of the smoking ban and the growth in home drinking has forced many pubs to reinvent themselves in order to survive. The Licensing Act of 2003 also changed many aspects of the traditional pub, particularly the old opening times of 11am-2.30pm and 6-11pm that had shaped the social lives of pub goers for generations. Now most pubs are open all day with some staying open later in the evening. These changes have helped to open up new opportunities, for instance with food being served all afternoon, and coffees and even breakfasts in the mornings. Food now accounts for 50% of the income in the Brewery's managed houses.

Family-friendly pubs are now the norm, rather than the exception. Some pubs have branched out by opening grocery shops or post offices on their premises, reinforcing their positions at the heart of their local communities. Others have concentrated on offering good value and quality accommodation, reprising the historic role of the inn, with an increasing number of bookings now being made online.

So what has happened specifically to the Brewery's pubs, inns and hotels in the last decade? Back in 2001, the Victoria Inn in Salcombe had just become the 152nd premises in the Brewery's estate (page 55). Ten years on, the estate stands at 168 houses, and this number is forever changing as the Brewery buys and sells pubs as market opportunities arise.

Continuing the expansion eastwards that began in the 1980s, most of the Brewery's recent acquisitions have been in Devon, with one – the Racehorse at Taunton – being in Somerset. Notable Devon houses to join the estate within the last decade include the Hope and Anchor at Hope Cove, the Masons Arms at Branscombe and the Three Crowns at Chagford.

The latest project, in summer 2011, has been the renovation of the derelict Old Market House in Brixham to become a family-friendly food-led venue in a prominent position on the quayside. It was the Brewery's first conversion of a redundant building since the Shipwrights, in a similar situation on the harbourside in Padstow, back in the 1960s.

Standards and skills have risen in all areas of running a pub in the last ten years: catering, hospitality, marketing and cellar management are all now seen as crucial skills for running a successful public house.

Illustration commissioned for the Great Western Hotel, Newquay, in 2011

A NEW MILLENNIUM BEGINS, 2001-2011

Meanwhile, investment in the Brewery's existing houses continues to make sure that they provide high standards, good value and a friendly welcome to locals and visitors alike. The Brewery's flagship hotel - the Great Western at Newquay - was refurbished in 2008, and a new 33-bedroom hotel extension to the County Arms in Truro opened in June 2011. All managed houses with rooms are assessed and graded by the 'Quality In Tourism' scheme.

Standards and skills have risen in all areas of running a pub in the last ten years: catering, hospitality, marketing and cellar management are all now seen as crucial skills for running a successful public house, alongside the more traditional but equally important characteristics of being a welcoming and friendly host, and a good listener.

These new skills are honed and supported by the St Austell Brewery training academy – a centre of excellence for training and development in the hospitality and licensed sector that is recognised nationally by the BII (British Institute of Innkeeping). Absolutely critical in maintaining the reputation of St Austell Brewery houses for the highest standards in beer is to be able to guarantee the quality of cask ales 'from grain to glass' – and to this end all the Brewery's pubs are now signed up to Cask Marque, the independent quality assessor which helps ensure pubs serve and keep their cask ales in top condition.

The County Arms, Truro

LOCAL FUNDRAISING

The St Austell Brewery Charitable Trust was launched in 2003 to provide a channel for pubs, Brewery staff and customers to raise money for charities and good causes throughout the South West.

Since then it has raised more than £300,000 and has supported many charities and individuals in need throughout Cornwall, Devon and Somerset.

Members of the Senior Management Team went 'Back to the Floor' and hosted a fundraising dinner at the Pescadou restaurant, Padstow

Merlin Crossingham of Aardman, Creative Director for Wallace and Gromit, at the Visitor Centre

Garvey Evans and his father Glyn receiving a donation from Viv May and Robin Freight

Ian Blunt and Danny Crabb with Lorna Baker of St Luke's Hospice in Plymouth

Jeremy Mitchell with Trevor Bould, Finance Director for Cornwall Hospice Care

SUPPLY & DELIVERY

Another major change in the life and fortunes of St Austell Brewery was the opening of the Cornwall Distribution Centre in January 2009.

For many decades, the Brewery's priority was to offer personal service to its customers in all parts of Cornwall and the Isles of Scilly through a network of seven small depots, but increasingly this had become an inefficient and expensive way of doing business.

With the locating of one very large distribution centre at St Columb, the largest single depot in Cornwall, the company has been able to run a more efficient distribution service, reduce road miles and improve load planning. The centre now stores all the Brewery's wines, spirits and soft drinks for all its customers in Cornwall, and many of those in Devon.

The company has been able to run a more efficient distribution service, reduce road miles and improve load planning.

A NEW MILLENNIUM BEGINS, 2001-2011

Welcoming visitors all year round

In 2001 the Brewery's Visitor Centre (see page 62) was, as we now know, still in its infancy. Since then there has been a major expansion of its role, recognising that people want to find out more, to discover the stories behind their favourite brews and favourite pubs, to explore one of Cornwall's oldest and most successful traditional businesses, as well as to buy, sample and relax. A new interactive museum opened in 2005, based on the Brewery's history as told in this book, and in 2010 the Wine Warehouse opened on the ground floor.

Now a member of the Cornwall Association of Tourist Attractions, the Visitor Centre serves traditional pub food and drink (including, of course, possibly the best pint of St Austell beer you'll ever taste),

and provides a welcoming destination throughout the year for shopping, eating, drinking, browsing and taking the ever-popular guided brewery tours. Indeed, the Hicks Bar at the heart of the Visitor Centre also provides a valuable social hub for Brewery staff, and visitors can rub shoulders with pensioners playing euchre on a Thursday lunchtime or with the brewing team and office workers relaxing over a welcome pint of Tribute on a Friday at the end of the working week.

To book guided tours or to enquire about hiring the Visitor Centre for meetings, conferences, parties or weddings, call 01726 66022 or go to www.staustellbrewery.co.uk

THE RETURN OF SMUGGLERS

Turn back to page 44 and you will read a heartfelt lament from a passionate and despairing fan of one of the Brewery's most infamous brews, which came to an end in 1994. It is a great joy to be able to report, however, that not all good things that come to an end come to an end for ever…

With the installation of the new bottling line, Smugglers was reborn, and this unique blend of dark ale and oak-aged barley wine returned to the stage with a vengeance.

Smugglers

Reinvigorated with a new recipe, the reborn Smugglers is a winning blend of oak-aged barley wine and dark ale brewed from natural Cornish spring water, Maris Otter pale ale malt, Crystal and Roasted malts, dark brewing sugar, First Gold, Fuggle, and Styrian Golding hops, coriander and our own Brewer's yeast. This strong beer is brewed and racked into oak whisky casks before being hidden away in our cellars. During its long slumber the beer undergoes an extraordinary transformation, emerging rich and complex with hints of whisky, creamy vanilla, toffee and spice.

Smugglers Grand Cru

For those who want something totally unique and even more powerful, the Brewery also introduced Smugglers Grand Cru, finished in the bottle using the Méthode Champenoise at the Camel Valley Vineyard in Cornwall. This exceptional brew was voted 'Champion Speciality Beer' at the 2011 Quality Drinks Awards.

All in all, that should be enough to make D.W.E. of Fowey happy, surely?

EXTRA STRONG

SMUGGLERS GRAND CRU

11.5% VOL

SUPERIOR OAK AGED STRONG ALE

TRAGEDY STRIKES THE PANDORA

On the peaceful yet breezy morning of March 24th 2011, following a few weeks of welcome spring sunshine, a terrible fire struck one of Cornwall's most iconic pubs in a freak incident.

The much-loved Pandora Inn, on the banks of the Fal estuary at Restronguet, is an ancient building with a famous thatched roof. Every morning the welcoming fires are lit in the bars, only on this day a rogue spark lit the thatch and within minutes the whole pub went up in flames. Luckily nobody was hurt, and this historic pub will be rebuilt.

LOCAL SOURCING FROM GRAIN TO GLASS

A recent development has seen Head Brewer Roger Ryman working with Tuckers Maltings of Newton Abbott to create a totally new malt, which they have called Cornish Gold.

Cornish Gold is made solely from barley that has been grown in Cornwall, and grown specifically to be used in brewing St Austell Brewery's own ales. At the last count six Cornish farms have started growing barley to feed the ever growing demand for Tribute Ale and St Austell's other beers.

THE GREENING OF THE BREWERY

The opening of the Cornwall Distribution Centre at St Columb clearly made good environmental sense, and this leads us to another key area of the Brewery's development in the past decade.

With the environment coming to the fore of the national political and social agenda, and Cornwall leading the way in innovation, technology and green thinking, the Brewery created and published its Environmental Policy in 2007. The policy covers all the diverse aspects of the company's business and commits it to reductions in carbon emissions, energy use and negative impact on the local environment. Since then, measures that have been put in place include the lagging of roofs, recycling throughout all Brewery sites, introducing lower weight glass in bottles and the development of a paper policy to use recycled paper.

The greatest accolade for St Austell Brewery in recent years was winning the prestigious Regional Brewer of the Year 2009 at the National Publican Awards.

This highly competitive award is presented each year to the regional brewery that can demonstrate excellence in both its retail and brewing operations.

The judges look for clear evidence of financial stability and success; an effective programme of staff training and development; marketing and promotional strategy; excellent standards of customer service; innovation; excellence in beer production and quality from brewery to glass; a unique selling point; and corporate social responsibility.

At the awards ceremony, they explained their choice of St Austell Brewery for the top prize: *'Strong growth in its core beer brand* [Tribute] *on a national scale has made St Austell the winner of Regional Brewer of the Year...Tribute is blossoming now to become a national brand. In a challenging market in 2008 St Austell Brewery has developed its pub estate so that it can trade excellently throughout the year within a market that is notoriously seasonal. Judges were impressed by a business that is well funded and structured, strengths which have enabled St Austell Brewery to invest in its estate, its people and its future.'*

James Staughton, in proudly accepting the award, acknowledged what is the enduring core strength of this remarkable company: *'Perhaps more than any other industry, our business is all about people and this award is a tribute to the whole team who work for and are involved with St Austell Brewery and our pub estate. It is also a great day for the South West and the principle that a family-owned, independent business from Cornwall can lead the way nationally.'*

'This award is a tribute to the whole team who work for and are involved with St Austell Brewery and our pub estate'

The Brewery team celebrating the award at The Hicks Bar

The UK's Best Managed Pub 2010, The Rashleigh Arms, Charlestown

A NEW MILLENNIUM BEGINS, 2001-2011

The family firm

James Staughton, Managing Director

And what of Walter Hicks's dynasty in this new millennium? As the original book drew to a close, we saw the retirement of Piers Thompson (who became non-executive Chairman) and his cousin Peter Voelcker, and the appointment of Walter's great-great grandson James Staughton as Managing Director in 2000 – the fifth generation of the Hicks family to be actively involved in running the Brewery.

James's cousin Gerard Barnes (grandson, like James, of Egbert Barnes) became a non-executive Director in 2005. In the following year, on his 70th birthday, Piers Thompson stood down as Chairman and was given the title of Honorary President. He was succeeded as non-executive Chairman by another of Walter Hicks's great-great grandsons –Will Michelmore, the great-grandson of Walter junior and Kattie Cooke. For a clearer picture, see the Hicks family tree on page 92 to discover how this new generation links back to the founding father of the Brewery.

In the meantime, Piers Thompson junior has been playing an active role in developing the Brewery's national sales department in his capacity as National Sales Manager. Based in London, he has helped to secure and increase Tribute sales in the Home Counties and the East of England.

Piers Thompson junior (right) celebrates Tribute being made available at The Mad Bishop and Bear, a Fullers pub, at Paddington Station

Humphrey Voelcker has just joined the Brewery as our Estate Surveyor having worked for Savills in London as an Associate within their Business Space Investment Team for ten years.

Of the other Brewery families, whose long association and loyalty and generations of service form part of the bedrock of this company and help to make it the thriving business that it is (see page 28 and elsewhere throughout the book), there are still Sprague, Soady, Saunders, Bray, Bone, Johns, Freight, Bassett, Orton, Poskitt, Raikes, Eade and Barrett; of those names more than one generation is currently working at the Brewery.

Loyalty and generations of service form part of the bedrock of this company and help to make it the thriving business that it is today.

Messages of Congratulations

Malcolm Bell
Head of Tourism, Visit Cornwall

'Tourism has been a major force in the economy of Cornwall and it provides hundreds of businesses with their income, as well as over 40,000 jobs for the people of Cornwall. Tourism is one of the most competitive industries in the world and the unique attraction of Cornwall has always been its environment and the quality of life we enjoy. At the heart of any community is the pub and out local beers and this is something very special . The Brewery has been at the heart of the development of new beers and a quality food offering in its pubs. Long may the brewery continue and I am sure the strong connection with tourism bodies will help us to grow from strength to strength.'

Anita George, MBE, JP
Tenant of The Logan Rock Inn & The Yacht Inn

'Our family has been connected with the brewery since 1982, during that time we have found friendship and sincerity from an amazingly run brewery. As a family we have gone from strength to strength, running two excellent houses namely The Yacht Inn at Penzance and The Logan Rock Inn at Treen. The support offered by St Austell Brewery is second to none, we have built up a wonderful relationship with the Brewery, Roger Ryman has certainly brewed some first class ales winning many awards. Our two sons Nicholas and Mark are also involved with our business, and join us in congratulating St Austell Brewery on their 160th Anniversary.'

Stephen Gilbert
Member of Parliament for St Austell & Newquay

'Over the last 160 years Cornwall has gone through huge change. Like tin mining in the west, the local clay mining industry in central Cornwall has reduced over time and other traditional industries, like farming and fishing, have seen times change too. In recent years we've seen a surge in new industries like renewable energy, exploiting Cornwall's wealth of natural resources, creative companies and services based firms moving to Cornwall to take advantage of the lifestyle and the UK's first super-fast broadband, as well as a steady growth in year-round high-end tourism.

'St Austell Brewery has provided a backdrop to all those changes and their ales have been the staple for many generations. We all have our favourite from the brewery and mine is Tribute. After being elected to Parliament I was delighted to be able to take a taste of Cornwall to the Members' Bar in the House of Commons – four barrels of Tribute went in just a couple of nights, a testament to its great taste. Here's to the next 160 years for one of St Austell's finest exports and best family businesses!'

Lady Mary Holborow DCVO, JP
Lord Lieutenant of Cornwall

'Once again I am delighted to be able to offer my congratulations to St Austell Brewery – this time on its 160th anniversary. St Austell Brewery is certainly one of the great institutions of Cornwall – producing excellent beer and giving employment to so many Cornish people. It plays a very important part in the life of Cornwall – both economically and giving so much pleasure to all those who appreciate visiting their pubs.

'With many congratulations to all the staff and tenants of such a very successful and much loved Cornish business.'

Kevin Lavery
Chief Executive, Cornwall Council

'There's no doubt that St Austell Brewery has a place close to every Cornish heart! It is certainly more than a simple brewery producing very fine ales; it is the epitome of a growing, modern and successful business that has used its historical connections to excellent effect. It has its roots in the local communities and does its very best to promote good quality and local service. Its reach across the whole of Cornwall has made it a very effective partner with the Council on the Clean Cornwall Campaign. I wish it every success over the next 160 years.'

Dave Linnell OBE
CEO and Principal, Cornwall College

'I would like to offer my congratulations to St Austell Brewery on this anniversary.

'As someone born and brought up in Cornwall, I feel privileged to be able to write a few words about St Austell Brewery. The Brewery has been an integral part of the life of Cornwall and has brought much credit to the County. As a regular consumer of its products it has traded on high quality food and drink and a superb ambiance to its public houses and hotels. I hope that the next 160 years are as successful as the last 160. My best wishes to everyone associated with this excellent business.'

Messages of Congratulations

Paul Nunny
Director, Cask Marque Trust

'St Austell is a company that is a shining example to the drinks industry on how to reinvent itself. From a brewery known and loved locally it is now recognised nationally through the success of Tribute, their cask ale created by Head Brewer, Roger Ryman.

'On this important side of the business they have won numerous national awards for their employee training programmes and have invested heavily in improving retailing standards.

'St Austell have endorsed and supported Cask Marque, custodians of beer quality in the industry. Apart from staff training this involves costly investment in cellars and dispense equipment so they can rightly be proud of the quality of their beers. Each year St Austell pubs are regularly and independently inspected by Cask Marque to ensure they serve a great pint. Congratulations to the company and its employees in securing the brewery's long term future.'

Alan Qualtrough
Editor of The Western Morning News

'Tribute was first brewed as Daylight Robbery to commemorate the 1999 solar eclipse, which was just before my arrival in the Westcountry from London to begin a new chapter in life.

'My first introduction to this distinctive and distinguished beer was in the taproom of St Austell Brewery following an invitation to meet the head brewer and the management team.

'As a newcomer to Cornwall and searching for clues to the region's identity the visit made a lasting impression; it was the sturdiness, the strength of character, the independence, the individuality yet 'connectedness' of the St Austell Brewery that inspired me.

'And Tribute with its special colour, aroma and taste encapsulated for me the bold and unique qualities of the brewery and of the wider region.

'Tribute became a favourite and as I travel to the county I look out for it as if it were a compass pointing the way home. So when drinking a pint of Tribute in Liverpool or Leicester or at the bar at Paddington Station it is never difficult to allow one's mind to wander and imagine gazing out of the window of a Cornish harbour-side pub and hearing the sound of screeching gulls.

'This is the epitome of a great brand, one that harnesses and stirs the emotions and reflects a certain quality - in this case Cornishness, its existence only possible through the thoughtful actions of a company rooted in its community and one that cares about its customers and its products.

'So well done to St Austell Brewery for making a proper job of success. Congratulations on 160 sparkling years with the hope of many, many more of your own chapters to come.'

Neil Robertson
Chief Executive to the British Institute of Innkeeping

'St Austell have been leaders in Corporate Social Responsibility long before it was even invented. Their commitment to and standards of training are nothing short of excellent. Corporately and individually they have received our highest awards.

'They support and develop their people and their community and are a real asset to Cornwall and the industry they are part of. In short, St Austell are grounded and rounded and a pleasure to work with.'

Alex Robertson
Leader of Cornwall Council

'As a former pub landlord I really appreciate the importance of the pub as a place where people can come together to talk, laugh and enjoy. St Austell Brewery has great pubs across the South West and the beer they produce has been welcomed with open arms right across the country.

'It's a great Cornish success story and the fact that they are now celebrating their 160th birthday is a testament to all the hard work that has gone into growing the brewery's business. What I am particularly impressed with is the way St Austell Brewery has never lost sight of the position the pub occupies at the heart of the community. The MD James Staughton's successful work in setting up the Clean Cornwall organisation shows just how much he and his company care about Cornwall and how they are prepared to invest time and money in promoting the area.

'The Brewery is a great ambassador for Cornwall and we are as proud of their achievements as they are of their great Cornish heritage. It is heartening to see the brewery continuing to thrive in the 21st century just as Cornwall is looking to the future with new investment in renewable energy and superfast broadband being installed across the area. Times change but we will always need a place to meet, relax, and discuss the great issues of the day.

'Happy Birthday St Austell Brewery and I'll be toasting your achievement with a fine pint of Tribute. Long may your success continue.'

Messages of Congratulations

Isaac Sheps
CEO, Carlsberg UK

'We are both honoured and privileged to be asked to provide a testimonial on the occasion of St Austell Brewery's 160 year celebration.

'Our two businesses were founded just four years apart and I'm delighted to say that over the last 160 years or so we have both gone from strength to strength.

'During the last 30 years we have been immensely proud of the partnership that has been developed between our two businesses. Like any strong partnership it is built upon shared values and beliefs, and a desire to create a win-win relationship for both parties.

'As a business one of our winning behaviours is "together we are stronger" and I can think of no greater example than our long standing relationship. There is in no doubt that in the South West we are stronger due to our partnership and I hope that St Austell would also feel the same.

'St Austell are not only our partners but have also provided inspiration in how to manage and operate a successful business in what remains a turbulent and challenging environment for both brewers and pubs.

'Our partnership with St Austell is one of the longest and most successful relationships we have, not only in the UK but across the world.

'Whilst obviously the celebration is about looking back, we also want to look forward to the next 160 years of success and we hope that we will enjoy it together.

'So for all the great work done by St Austell and all of the people who have worked for the business during the last 160 years, I definitely state "That Calls for a Carlsberg".'

'St Austell are not only our partners but have also provided inspiration in how to manage and operate a successful business in what remains a turbulent and challenging environment for both brewers and pubs.' Isaac Sheps, CEO, Carlsberg UK

Brigid Simmonds OBE
Chief Executive, British Beer and Pub Association

'The British Beer and Pub Association welcomes the opportunity to pay "Tribute" to St Austell Brewery – one of our founding members with a long and proud history not only of excellence in brewing and hospitality – but also in its contribution to its local community and to tourism in Cornwall.

'For 160 years this family enterprise has supported hundreds of jobs across Cornwall, provided a welcome economic contribution and added value to the Cornish experience. From Clouded Yellow to Proper Job, from Admirals Ale to the new Korev: this beacon of brewing is something of which we are all proud. The future of the industry depends on partnerships and St Austell's contribution to "Newquay Safe", working with the police and local authority, is a real example of best practice. At the BBPA we are delighted to have St Austell as a member – we look forward to their continued membership for the next 160 years.'

Daphne Skinnard
BBC Radio Cornwall

'St Austell is one of the things that makes life in Cornwall such fun. From the cliff tops at Treen to the coastal inlet at Restronguet, it's always enjoyable to introduce visitors to the lovely locations, interesting local flavour and genuine Cornish hospitality of a St Austell pub. St Austell Brewery is an impressive example of a local specialist surviving and prospering in an increasingly faceless and corporate world. This is still relevant a decade on and I would like to say an enormous congratulations to everyone for their 160th birthday.'

Tim Smit
Chief Executive, Eden Project

'Wherever you are in Cornwall you are never far from a St Austell House. There's something deeply comforting about the name, as if it stood for virtues as deeply rooted in Cornwall as the granite from which most of the ale houses were built. It's not fussy, or trendy, in fact it's reassuringly old-fashioned. This is staff of life stuff, not designer froth.

'The HQ in St Austell is austere and unforgiving with no concession to frills, its prison-like quality appropriate to the names of its famous brews: Tinners, Wreckers, Daylight Robbery etc. Most importantly, it sits on the bluff above the once quaint market and mining town that gave it its name.

Messages of Congratulations

The brewery gives the place a character and connection with the past that compensates, in some small part, for the ache of bereavement through the last fifty years as first tin and then clay began their contraction.

'That was many pints ago, now we have a bright future to look forward to and I would like to wish all at St Austell Brewery well as they seek to uphold a name of which they can be justly proud.

'I wrote these words 10 years ago since then the famous old brewery has maintained its values, but it has created a magnificent ale – Tribute, which has won it new fans across the country and, dare I say it, made it, almost, trendy. We need now to be watchful and secretive lest one of Cornwall's great treasures is discovered by too many others...ah well, if it had to happen – you can't keep quality down and rightly so. Many congratulations at reinventing yourselves without losing your heart. Here's to another 160.'

'St Austell is a company that is a shining example to the drinks industry on how to reinvent itself. From a brewery known and loved locally it is now recognised nationally through the success of Tribute.'

Paul Nunny, Director, Cask Marque Trust

Rick Stein
Seafood Chef & Restaurateur

'Most of my life has memories of St Austell Brewery. Like most of us who were children in the '50s it's sitting in the back of my parents car in the pub car park with a bottle of their Ginger Beer and a packet of crisps with the salt in the blue waxed paper. The label on the Ginger Beer was of the white pyramids of waste from the China Clay pits, the idea of using an illustration of what was essentially industrial waste on a label I think is now rather sweetly innocent. Then probably at about 17 tripping into a Cornish hedge outside the Farmer's Arms in St Merryn after my first pint of half and half (Ordinary and Extra) and now after years of stoutly defending, perhaps not the best beer in the world as my favourite I can proudly say in our pub that Cornish ales are genuinely the best. I am so amazingly proud that our local beers are so very good and the brewery is so excitingly dynamic.'

Piers Thompson
Honorary President, St Austell Brewery

'As one of the last serving members of the fourth generation of the Hicks family I am honoured to have been asked in my capacity as President to write a few words.

'I have no doubt that Walter Hicks would have been proud and delighted with the remarkable growth in sales of our own beer in the ten years since our 150th anniversary in 2001.

'To the fifth generation led by William Michelmore and James Staughton and all who work for the Brewery I wish good luck and continued success in the years to come.'

Tim Thornton
The Bishop of Truro

'I was delighted to have a tour of the brewery as part of a visit I was doing along with my Methodist colleague to St Austell recently. I am very grateful to have this opportunity to send my congratulations to the St Austell Brewery on its 160th anniversary. I found the staff incredibly friendly and the atmosphere very warm indeed. It is wonderful that the brewery goes from strength to strength and just as churches are clearly at the heart of the village, so also pubs are very important community resources. I am therefore delighted to offer my congratulations to all concerned for the fact that the St Austell Brewery is a wonderful example of a company that is sustainable, rooted in the local community and constantly aware of the need to develop in the future.'

Simon Townsend
Chairman, Cornwall Association of Tourist Attractions

'St Austell Brewery has a reputation for excellence from its fine ales to the fantastic visitor centre and brewery tours.

'A pint of Tribute when on holiday in Cornwall is an absolute must.

'Cornwall is very lucky to have such a large independent brewer that also owns and operates many fine Pubs, Inns and Hotels.

'The Cornwall Association of Tourist Attractions (CATA) is proud that St Austell Brewery's Visitor Centre is a member of the Association.'

Brewery Staff 2011

150th anniversary message from
HRH Prince Charles, the Duke of Cornwall

(his Foreword to the original 2001 book Brewing for Cornwall)

ST. JAMES'S PALACE

As one of a small number of independent family brewers left in Britain, the St Austell Brewery has grown steadily from the initial vision of a young Cornishman called Walter Hicks in 1851 to become one of the largest private companies in Cornwall. With its distinctive black and gold paintwork adorning its public houses, and the historic brewery itself up on the hill above St Austell still brewing beers known to earlier generations, St Austell Brewery has become part of the fabric of Cornwall.

The Company makes a notable contribution to the rural communities of Cornwall - and Devon - through its ownership of local pubs and its investment in their future. It has played its part in the local economy for over 150 years as a large and reliable employer and represents, with its continuing emphasis on the quality of hospitality, an important contribution to the tourist industry on which Cornwall relies so heavily.

On the occasion of St Austell Brewery's 150th anniversary, I would like to send my congratulations to its staff, management and tenants, all of whom form part of a great Cornish success story.

Appendix I
Directors of the Company

Walter Hicks	1910/16	Chairman		
Walter Hicks junior	1910/11			
Hester Parnall	1911/39	Chairman 1916/39		
Reginald Barnes	1916/35			
Christopher Ellis	1934/50			
Egbert Barnes	1935/79	Chairman 1939/79	President 1979/87	
Kenneth Moore	1939/76			
Arthur Payne	1939/42	Managing		
Claude Aylwin	1942/47	Managing		
Scott Seaward	1944/60			
George Luck	1948/79	Managing		
Leonard Minchin	1952/57			
David Payne	1959/63			
Ian Turnbull	1961/63			
David Staughton	1963/2000	Chairman 1979/2000		
Piers Thompson	1967/2007	Managing 1979/2000	Chairman 2000/2007	President 2007/
Peter Voelcker	1967/2008			
Michael Ruthven	1987/2000			
Adam Luck	1988/			
James Staughton	1988/	Managing 2000/		
William Michelmore	1996/	Chairman 2008/		
Jonathan Neame	2002/			
Gerard Barnes	2005/			

Bold type: Members of the Hicks family

Appendix II
Hicks Family Tree

WALTER HICKS 1829/1916

m.(1858)
Emma Andrew
1830/1863

m.(1864)
Caroline Andrew
1838/1901

Emma
1859/1951

Clara
1860/1961

Walter
1865/1911
m.(1890)
Kattie Cooke
1857/1905

Hester
1866/1939
m.(1905)
Thomas Parnall
1839/1915

Corona
1891/1959

Gerald
1893/1915

Stella
1896/1984
m.(1923)
Bernard Harvey
1888/1973

Viola
1899/1976
m.(1926)
William Baseden
1898/1978

Corona, Gerald, Stella and Viola

June
1924/
m.(1953)
James Michelmore
1924/

Timothy
1928/
m.(1954)
Susan Michelmore
1931/

Gerald
1927/
m.(1952)
Margaret Pratt
1930/

Shirley
1929/2009
m.(1952)
William Harper
1926/1997

Kate
1956/
m.(1983)
John
Kelleher
1953/

Robert
1957/
m.(1987)
Susan
Lodge
1960/

William
1959/
m.(1990)
Jacqueline
Mapeldoram
1965/

Peter
1955/
m.(1977)
Angela
Firth
1955/

m.(2005)
Julia
Webb
1968/

Penelope
1956/
Ben
Campbell
1957/

Isobel
1961/
Simon
Kosminsky
1958/

Tamsin
1963/
m.(1992)
Peter
Brewer
1957/

Catherine
1953/
m.(1973)
Michael
Morris
1953/

Sarah
1955/
m.(1977)
Michael
Vandenbraak
1951/1999

m.(1984)
Henry
Hart III
1950/

Jennifer
1956/
m.(1975)
David Kull
1956/

m.(1984)
Douglas
Hochuli
1952/

Steven
1958/
m.(1980)
Maylene
Otsuji
1961/

Judith
1963/
m.(1985)
John
Heffernan
1963/

Alan
1964/
m.(1995)
Debra
Eisenbach
1967/

Linden
1953/
m.(1980)
Nicholas
Jones
1952/

m.(1996)
Roy
Lambden
1946/

Simon
1954/
m.(1980)
Sharon
Connolly
1956/

Matthew
1958/
m.(1983)
Sandra
Bishop
1950/

m.(1994)
Hazel
Secker
1952/

Sarah
1987/

William
1989/

Richard
1993/

Clare
1991/

Andrew
1993/

Thomas
1995/

Harry
1997/

Thomas
1979/

Mary
1982/

Laurie
1994/

Emma
1988/

Michael
1991/

Sam
1994/

James
1996/

Carolyn
1978/

Elizabeth
1983/

Marianne
1985/

Jaquelyn
1979/

Richard
1984/

Alexander
1987/

Tessa
1989/

Matthew
1986/

Kevin
1989/

Christy
1981/

Kimberley
1983/

Steven
1996/

Dillon
1985/

Emma
1996/

Ethan
1998/

William
1981/

Virginia
1985/
m.(2011)
Rory
Green
1978/

Laura
1984/

Jovin
1986/

Bradley
1979/

Jay
1984/

Benjamin
1991/

Bold type: members of the Hicks family directly involved in the management of the Brewery.

Walter Hicks and some of his daughters

Mary Hicks and Reginald Barnes's Wedding

Mary
1869/1954
m.(1896)
Reginald G Barnes
1869/1935

Susan
1870/1945

Caroline
1872/1954

Margaret
1873/1957

Kate
1875/1955
m.(1907)
Jack Hoyle
1882/1962

George
1880/1954
m.(1917)
Nancy Sr-de-Croix
1877/1967

Egbert
1898/1987
m.(1934)
Ruth Blezard
1901/1981

Hester
1900/1988
m.(1931)
Piers Thompson
1893/1969

Elizabeth
1904/1999
m.(1934)
George Fraser
1887/1970

Ruth
1910/1987
m.(1935)
Paul Voelcker
1901/1959

Gillian
1930
m.(1955)
Rodney Curry
1928

Richard
1932/1993
m.(1958)
Jacqueline Luke
1938

Olivia
1936/
m.(1957)
David Staughton
1931/

David
1940/
m.(1965)
Ursula Pitman
1944/

Roger
1933/2011
m.(1959)
Suzanne Holmes
1934/

m.(1986)
Margaret
Wood
1948/

Deborah
1936/
m.(1966)
David Varden
1927/

Piers
1937/
m.(1966)
Victoria Thwaites
1944/

Robert
1935/
m.(1964)
Sarah Peck
1941/

Patrick
1938/
m.(1975)
Patricia Frost
1948/

Peter
1938/
m.(1978)
Alison Edwards
1948/

Celia
1943/
m.(1982)
James Milnes Gaskell
1937/

Rosemary
1947/

Patrick
1956/
m.(1979)
Amanda
Jane Scott
1956/

Alexandra
1960/

Tessa
1961/
m.(1986)
Peter
Stock
1959/

Ben
1964/
m.(1990)
Tracy
Bayliss
1962/

Virginia
1969/

Julia
1962/
m.(1991)
Michael
Clancy
1962/

Alexander
1966/

Thomas
1969/

James
1959/
m.(1995)
Rebecca
Trafford
1963/

m.(2000)
Emma
Minter-Kemp
1960/

Julia
1960/

Fiona
1963/
m.(1991)
Clive
Roberts
1958/

Gerard
1968/
m.(1996)
Jane
Larroucau
1968/

Robert
1969/

Adam
1959/
Jessica
Datta
1952/

Lucy
1962/

Hugo
1966/
Sophie
Friend
1963/

Clara
1988/

Richard
1967/
m.(1998)
Ashley
Cameron
1972/

James
1969/
m.(1998)
Janine
Anketell
1967/

Annabel
1968/
m.(1998)
Jonty
White
1965/

Piers
1971/
m.(2010)
Emma
Blaney
1983/

Emily
1983/
m.(2009)
Rupert
Burnell-
Nugent
1982/

Fiona
1965/

David
1966/

Alexandra
1979/

Camilla
1981/

Sophie
1981/

Humphrey
1980/

Arthur
1988/

Charles
1983/

Anna
1985/

James
1981/

Charlotte
1983/

Felix
1987/

India
1994/

Milo
1999/

Torran
2000/

Jack
1994/

Finn
1997/

Oscar
1999/

Sabine
1998/

Emma
2000/

Olivia
1993/

Katrina
1996/

Christian
1998/

Benedict
2000/

Celeste
1988/

Coralie
1991/

Alexander
2000/

Amelia
2003/

John
2002/

Harriet
2005/

Archie
1999/

Matilda
2001/

Emma Hicks, Hester Parnall
and Walter Hicks junior

Mary Barnes and
her daughter Hester

Appendix III
Pubs and hotels owned by the Brewery in 2011

Name	Date Acquired	Name	Date Acquired
Abbey Inn, Buckfast	1996	**Crown Inn**, Goldsithney	1911
Angarrack Inn, Hayle	1935	**Crown Inn**, St Ewe	1917
Atlantic Hotel, Isles of Scilly	2003	**Crows Nest**, Darite (formerly Sun Inn)	1905
Atlantic Inn, Isles of Scilly	1988		
Badger Inn, Lelant (formerly Lelant Hotel)	1935	**Dolphin**, Exeter (formerly Tap and Barrel)	1994
Barley Sheaf, Bodmin	1898	**Dolphin Inn**, Grampound	1916
Barley Sheaf, Liskeard	1910	**Dolphin Tavern**, Penzance	1935
Bettle & Chisel Inn, Delabole (formerly Delabole Inn)	1925	**Duke of Cornwall**, St Austell	1889
		Earl of Chatham, Lostwithiel	1926
Bishop & Wolf Inn, Isles of Scilly	1958	**Earl of St Vincent**, Egloshayle	1922
Blue Anchor, Fraddon	1939	**Edgcumbe Arms**, Cremyll	1994 (Leasehold)
Borough Arms, Bodmin	2009	**Eliot Arms**, St Germans	2007 (Leasehold)
Brass Monkey, Teignmouth	1996	**Falcon Inn**, St Mawgan	1988 (Leasehold)
Buccaneer Inn, Torquay	1996	**Falmouth Arms**, Ladock	1893
Bucket of Blood, Phillack	1935	**Farmers Arms**, St Merryn	1951
Bugle Inn, Bugle	1920 (Freehold 1971)	**Ferryboat Inn**, Helford Passage	1987 (Leasehold)
Carbeile Inn, Torpoint	1984	**Fire Engine**, Marazion	1935
Carlyon Arms, St Austell	1929	**Fishermans Arms**, Newlyn	1935
Castle Inn, Lydford	2008	**Fishermans Arms**, Plymouth	1991
Cellars Bar, Teignmouth	1996	**Fort Inn**, Newquay	1997
Central Inn, Newquay	1902	**Fountain Inn**, Mevagissey	1883
Church House Inn, Churchstow	2005	**Fountain Tavern**, Penzance	1935
Copley Arms, Hessenford	1959	**Four Lords**, St Blazey Gate	1904
Cornish Arms, Hayle	1935	**Four Winds**, Falmouth	1954
Cornish Arms, St Merryn	1926 (Freehold 1982)	**Fox & Hounds**, Comford	1949
Cornubia Hotel, Hayle	1935	**Globe Hotel**, Bude	1905 (Leasehold)
County Arms, Truro	2001	**Golden Lion**, Menherion	1923
Cromwell Arms, Bovey Tracey	2002	**Golden Lion**, Port Isaac	1922
Crown Hotel, Lynton	2006	**Great Western Hotel**, Newquay	1985

Name	Date Acquired	Name	Date Acquired
Grenville Arms, Nanpean	1911 (Freehold 1984)	**Mill on the Exe**, Exeter	1994
Harbour Inn, Padstow	1922	**Molesworth Arms**, Wadebridge	2006
Harbour Inn, Porthleven	1985	**Mount Ambrose Inn**, Mount Ambrose	1935
Hawkins Arms, Probus	1919	**Napoleon Inn**, Boscastle	1993
Heron Inn, Malpas	1930	**New Inn**, Park Bottom	1935
Hewas Inn, Sticker	1927	**New Inn**, Tywardreath	1932
Holly Tree Inn, Exmouth	2009	**New Inn**, Veryan	1943
Holmbush Inn, St Austell	1929	**North Inn**, Pendeen	1935
Hop & Vine, St Austell (formerly Sun Inn and O'Callaghan's)	1909	**Norway Inn**, Perranarworthal	2001
Hope & Anchor, Hope Cove	2006	**Old Custom House**, Padstow	1989
Jubilee Inn, Pelynt	2003	**Old Inn**, Mullion	2006
King of Prussia, Fowey	1895 (Freehold 1986)	**Old Market House**, Brixham	2011 (Leasehold)
Kings Arms, Bridges	1909	**Old Smithy**, Ivybridge	1996
Kings Arms, Lostwithiel	1922	**Old Success Inn**, Sennen	2008
Kings Arms, Marazion	1935	**Oyster Catcher Bar**, Polzeath (formerly Polzeath Hotel)	1963
Kings Arms, Paul	1935	**Pandora Inn**, Restronguet Creek	1982
Kings Arms, St Just	1935	**Par Inn**, Par	1926
Kings Arms, St Stephen	1915 (Freehold 1927)	**Paris Hotel**, Coverack	2009
Kings Arms, Tregony	2005	**Pedn-Olva Hotel**, St Ives	1999
Kings Head, Lane	2000	**Pityme Inn**, Pityme	1998
Lanivet Inn, Bodmin	1893	**Plume of Feathers**, Portscatho	1921
Lemon Arms, Mylor	1920	**Polgooth Inn**, Polgooth	1916
Lifeboat Inn, St Ives	1964 (Freehold 1997)	**Port William Inn**, Trebarwith Strand	2005
Logan Rock Inn, Treen	1958 (Freehold 1991)	**Punchbowl & Ladle**, Feock	2001
London Inn, Padstow	1907	**Queens Head**, St Stephen	1919
Lugger Inn, Fowey	1930 (Freehold 1989)	**Queens Hotel**, St Ives	1967
Lugger Inn, Polruan	1938	**Racehorse Inn**, Taunton	2008
Masons Arms, Branscombe	2010	**Radjel Inn**, Pendeen (formerly Boscaswell Inn)	1935
Masons Arms, Camelford	1923		

Appendix III
Pubs and hotels owned by the Brewery in 2011

Name	Date Acquired	Name	Date Acquired
Railway Inn, Illogan	1935	**Tap & Barrel**, Plymouth	2001
Rashleigh Arms, Charlestown	2002	**Tavern Inn**, Newquay	2007
Ring of Bells, Bishopsteignton	1966	**Ten Tors Inn**, Kingsteignton	2007
Rising Sun, St Mawes	1930	**Three Crowns Hotel**, Chagford	2009
Rodney Inn, Helston	1935	**Top House**, Lizard	2009
Rolle Quay Inn, Barnstaple	2000	**Travellers Rest**, Trevarrian	1935
Royal Standard, Hayle	1935	**Turnpike Inn**, Connor Downs	1935
Russell Inn, Polruan	1925	**Tyacks Hotel**, Camborne	1917
Safe Harbour, Fowey (formerly Commercial Hotel)	1903 (Freehold 1982)	**Victoria Inn**, Roche	1943
		Victoria Inn, Salcombe	2001
Sawles Arms, Carthew	1919	**Victoria Inn**, Threemilestone	1944
Seven Stars Inn, St Austell	1863 (Freehold 1925)	**Waterfront**, Plymouth	1998 (Leasehold)
Seven Stars Inn, Stithians	2007	**Watering Hole**, Plymouth	2010
Sharksfin, Mevagissey	2007	**Weavers**, Bodmin	1983
Sheaf of Wheat, St Ives	1904	**Welcome Home Inn**, Par	1913
Ship Hotel, Looe	1960	**Wellington Hotel**, St Just	1935
Ship Inn, Fowey	1891 (Freehold 1989)	**Western Hotel**, St Ives	1948
Ship Inn, Mevagissey	1896	**Western Inn**, St Austell	1943 (Freehold 1962)
Ship Inn, Mousehole	1901	**Westward Inn**, Lee Mill	1996
Ship Inn, Pentewan	1943	**White Hart Hotel**, Modbury	2010
Ship Inn, Portloe	1909 (Freehold 1947)	**White Hart Hotel**, St Austell	1911
Shipwrights, Padstow	1965	**White Horse Inn**, Launceston	2004
Sir Humphry Davy, Penzance (formerly St John's House)	1910	**Who'd Have Thought It Inn** St Dominick	2005
Sloop Inn, Bantham	2006	**Wig & Pen**, Truro (formerly Star Inn)	1926
St Agnes Hotel, St Agnes (formerly Paull's Hotel)	1923		
St Kew Inn, St Kew	1922	**William Cookworthy**, St Austell	1969
Star Inn, St Just	1935 (Freehold 1979)	**William IV**, Truro	1898
Swan Hotel, Wadebridge (formerly Commercial Hotel)	1922	**Wodehouse Arms**, Falmouth	1913
		Yacht Inn, Penzance	1935